YOUR SPIRITUAL MAKEOVER

EXPERIENCE THE BEAUTY OF A BALANCED LIFE— SPIRIT, SOUL AND BODY

By
Taffi L. Dollar

Harrison House
Tulsa, Oklahoma

10 09 08 07   10 9 8 7 6 5 4 3 2 1

Your Spiritual Makeover
Experience the Beauty of a Balanced Life—Spirit, Soul and Body
ISBN 13: 978-1-57794-914-5
ISBN 10: 1-57794-914-5
Copyright © 2007 by Taffi L. Dollar
P.O. Box 490124
College Park, GA 30349

Published by Harrison House, Inc.
P.O. Box 35035
Tulsa, Oklahoma 74153
harrisonhouse.com

TABLE OF CONTENTS

PREFACE

In my walk with the Lord, seeking His will for my life and desiring to be more like Him, the same issue has arisen again and again. I have found that how I arrange my life today, the priorities I set will determine who I am and what I'm doing the next day, and the days after that. My priorities determine my future, my state of mind—and whether I will experience the beauty of a balanced life.

An imbalanced life is marked by all the negative attributes of turmoil, instability, fear, selfishness, weakness and a lack of productivity. A balanced life includes a multitude of godly attributes: peace in the midst of the storm, a grateful and compassionate heart, wisdom and strength for the challenges of life and much fruit. But to have these godly attributes, we have to have our priorities lined up with God's priorities.

If we want to live a balanced life, we must set godly priorities.

What is a priority? A priority is that which is of first importance. Priorities are those things that we place a higher value on and attempt to attain or to fulfill in the course of our daily lives more than anything else. We can tell what our real priorities are by taking a good look at what we are doing with most of our time (and especially our free time), what we talk about most and what we think about most. I'm going to share some things with you that will help you to set your priorities according to God's Word, which means you may have to change the way you think, speak and act!

Jesus lived a perfectly balanced life, so our priorities need to be His priorities.

If we want our lives to reflect Jesus, then what is most important to Him must become what is most important to us. Making His priorities our priorities will bring to our lives the results He had in His life and in His ministry. Setting godly priorities is like opening the doors of our lives to Jesus and saying, "My life is completely Yours! What is most important for us to do today?"

We are living in the final hour before Jesus returns, getting down to the very last minutes on God's time clock. And if you are like me, you do not want to waste one moment. In order to do that, we need to line up our priorities with what the Word of God and the Spirit of God are saying to us. So I encourage you to do that by beginning *Your Spiritual Makeover* today— and *Experience the Beauty of a Balanced Life in 40 Days!*

Day 1

BEGIN WITH WELL-BALANCED CHOICES

Everything is permissible (allowable and lawful) for me; but not all things are helpful (good for me to do, expedient and profitable when considered with other things). Everything is lawful for me, but I will not become the slave of anything or be brought under its power.

1 Corinthians 6:12 AMP

From time to time it is a wonderful thing to confront ourselves and see where we are in God. Then we can make the changes we need to make so He can continue to take us to places in Him we have never been before, and show us things we have never seen before. He can unlock mysteries, give us new strategies to fulfill our callings, and free us from old ways of thinking and doing that have kept us from enjoying our lives in Him.

When you begin to set priorities according to God's Word, you will find you are doing a lot of fine-tuning. As 1 Corinthians 6:12 above says, we have tremendous freedom in Jesus, but we want to make the best choices instead of mediocre or bad choices. We certainly don't want to become a slave of anything or anyone—except Jesus.

As I have pressed into a higher dimension in God, there have been various things that I have had to lay aside. These things were not sinful or evil; however, they were not adding to my spiritual life and were causing imbalance in my walk with the Lord. When I am balanced, I walk with confidence and strength. However, when I allow things in my life that cause imbalance, my walk becomes unsteady and indecisive. It is hard to make right and good choices when I am staggering around, wondering which way is the best way to go.

I began to understand I was choosing to allow fear to come into my life and get me off balance. I knew how to cast off fear, and as I prioritized my life, I realized I was wasting my time and energy getting rid of fear I could have avoided in the first place. For example, I used to sit up and watch movies about serial killers! Of course, this often caused me to have nightmares about somebody chasing me and trying to kill me. At that time I didn't mind the nightmares; however, one day I realized I couldn't go where God wanted me to go and continue having them.

God wanted me to have sweet sleep and to be completely refreshed when I awoke. Therefore, I chose to lay aside what I was giving my eyes to, what I was giving my mind to, and what

I was allowing to come into my heart that was causing fearful dreams. I wasn't trying to be super-spiritual and religious; I just wanted to continue growing strong in God. He meant more to me than scary movies.

The Amplified Bible says that "everything is permissible." Watching movies is not bad; however, we want to make sure movies don't have any rule over our lives. The verse also says, "I will not become the slave of anything or be brought under its power." Although I did not feel like I was a slave to these scary movies, and I knew my authority in Jesus over any fear they caused, when the Holy Spirit impressed me to give them up, I knew they were a weight I needed to lay aside.

Another example of something being lawful but not expedient is when we adopt the lifestyle and habits of ministers and other Believers. We emulate them because we look up to them, and then we wonder why we don't see the same results in our lives. Even though imitating other strong Christians can bring some good perspectives and habits into our lives, eventually we find out that in order to be where God wants us to be, we have to live our lives the way He wants us to live them. It isn't that what other Believers are doing is bad; it is just that what they are doing is not what God wants us to be doing.

Other Believers may be able to watch movies about serial killers. It could be God has called them into professions where the information in these movies would give them insight and wisdom, so they don't put *them* off balance. They were not for me! If I modeled my life after those Believers' lives, my walk with the Lord would be hindered. Therefore, it is really important for us to follow the path God has set for us.

First Corinthians 6:12 gives us an important key to setting our priorities in a godly way. The apostle Paul tells us that in the freedom we have in Jesus Christ, we also have His wisdom to choose what is best for our lives.

REFRESH TODAY'S PRIORITIES

His mercies are new every morning!

Take a moment and ask the Holy Spirit to show you anything in your life that might be lawful and permissible, but not expedient and profitable. Then ask Him how to eliminate it from your life. In most cases He will want to replace it with something else that will prove helpful and fruitful. Remember, Jesus gave you the Holy Spirit to guide you, teach you and comfort you. With His help you are able to choose what's best!

Day 2

Enriched by Esteeming God

> By him were all things created, that are in heaven, and that are in earth, visible and invisible, whether they be thrones, or dominions, or principalities, or powers: all things were created by him, and for him:
>
> And he is before all things, and by him all things consist.
>
> And he is the head of the body, the church: who is the beginning, the firstborn from the dead; that in all things he might have the preeminence.
>
> Colossians 1:16-18

Do you believe what you just read? If you do, then your life should reflect "the preeminence" of Jesus Christ. He created you. He created the Earth and every material thing you enjoy. He redeemed you from sin and gave you His righteousness, peace, and joy in the Holy Ghost. He is the Head of the Church and His Body, of which you are a vital member. He holds the universe together—a perfect picture of balance—and He will hold your life together if you will let Him!

Colossians 1:16 also says we were created for Him. We are here on Earth for His pleasure and for His purpose. This verse tells me that before I was born, even before He created the heavens and the Earth, Jesus mapped out a set course and plan for me to discover and walk in, which is far better than what I could ever desire for myself. What this means in everyday, practical terms is that I often have to lay aside my own opinions and plans to subject everything to His will and plan for my life. I must continually recognize that Jesus is the final authority.

I have learned that esteeming God is not about going through a religious ritual a few times a week or saying long prayers before bedtime. We honor and esteem God when He is woven into everything we think, say and do. He has first place and is the primary influence in our lives every hour of the day—from the moment we awake in the morning—and through every hour while we are asleep. We are always conscious of and subject to His desires and His will. His Word and His Spirit are at the core of everything that concerns us or influences us.

If we don't keep God first and foremost in what we do, it is so easy to get off course by all kinds of distractions. We can avoid this by first setting aside time every day to spend with God and no one else and then stay in continuous communication with Him throughout the day. We cannot limit our time with Him to a two-hour church service on Sunday morning and an hour or two on Wednesday evening and then do anything we want to do the rest of the time. We may set priorities, but they will probably not be of God! We don't know His will if we don't talk with Him, and we won't stay in His will if we don't stay in communication with Him.

If we don't set the priorities in our lives, circumstances and people will. Setting priorities begins with esteeming God before anything or anyone else. The Bible talks about how the Macedonian Believers did this even as they were dealing with very hard times.

> **Moreover, brethren, we do you to wit of the grace of God bestowed on the churches of Macedonia;**
>
> **How that in a great trial of affliction the abundance of their joy and their deep poverty abounded unto the riches of their liberality.**
>
> **For to their power, I bear record, yea, and beyond their power they were willing of themselves;**
>
> **Praying us with much intreaty that we would receive the gift, and take upon us the fellowship of the ministering to the saints.**
>
> **And this they did, not as we hoped, but first gave their own selves to the Lord, and unto us by the will of God.**
>
> **2 Corinthians 8:1-5**

The Macedonian Believers were going through a "great trial of affliction" and "deep poverty." Yet, they had an abundance of joy. How did they do that? The answer is found in verse 5, which says that they "first gave their own selves to the Lord." They esteemed Him above and through all they were experiencing in their lives. Isn't it amazing that, with everything they were going through and all that was going on around them, they remained devoted to and focused on the Lord? Instead of getting entangled in all their problems and saying, "You know, it's hard to live right when you don't have money and you're being persecuted for your faith," they gave themselves to Jesus.

We are not supposed to give ourselves to situations, people and material things. We are to give ourselves to the Lord. He doesn't tell us to do this to make our lives miserable. He tells us to do this so that we can have the abundance of joy the Macedonians had!

If we don't esteem God by giving ourselves fully to Him all day long, our lives can dry up and wither. We cannot bear fruit because we have stopped the daily flow of His love, life, power and authority in our lives. When we give ourselves to Him, all these things flow through us and we can be everything He's called us to be to everyone He wants us to touch.

God wants to bless you! He wants you to have abundance of joy even when you are facing terrific challenges in your life.

The sure way to get in the mighty outpouring of His blessings is to honor and to esteem Him by putting Him first and consulting Him first, at all times and in all situations.

REFRESH TODAY'S PRIORITIES

His mercies are new every morning!

Throughout your day today, keep track of what you think about. Are you giving the Lord your undivided attention whenever possible? Do you consult Him as you make all the little decisions as well as the big decisions? Whether you are a busy professional or a wife and mother going in five directions at the same time, you can train yourself to meditate on God's Word and commune with the Holy Spirit. This is esteeming God in your life.

Day 3

An Essential Eternal Perspective

Heaven and earth shall pass away, but my words shall not pass away.

Matthew 24:35

This world is going to pass away one day. Those who live for the world and are attached to everything in it, who find their pleasure and security in physical things, do not have much to look forward to! There is only one thing in this world that will never pass away: the Word of God. Everything in the Bible will stand forever, so if we want our lives to count for something for eternity, we should base them on God's Word.

The day of the Lord will come as a thief in the night; in the which the heavens shall pass away with a great noise, and the elements shall melt with fervent heat, the earth also and the works that are therein shall be burned up.

Seeing then that all these things shall be dissolved, what manner of persons ought ye to be in all holy conversation and godliness?

2 Peter 3:10-11

Having an eternal perspective brings balance to your life by revealing what your priorities should be. Knowing that one day your house, your car, your clothes, your jewelry and all your toys and games will perish—everything but God's Word will be completely destroyed by fire—what should you do today? Peter is telling us not only that all the material things of this world are temporary, he is also giving us a truth upon which we should live our lives. Let's look at all of verse 11 and continue with what Peter has to say.

Seeing then that all these things shall be dissolved, what manner of persons ought ye to be in all holy conversation and godliness,

Looking for and hasting unto the coming of the day of God, wherein the heavens being on fire shall be dissolved, and the elements shall melt with fervent heat?

Nevertheless we, according to his promise, look for new heavens and a new earth, wherein dwelleth righteousness.

2 Peter 3:11-13

We should never allow the world to dictate how we live our lives. We must always look to God's Word. When God's Word is our final authority in all matters and issues, then we will always be conscious of eternity. We will have an eternal perspective on everything because God's Word is the one thing that will last forever!

The world doesn't even want to think about the last days and the destruction of the heavens and the Earth because they live in constant fear of eternity. They fear it because they will be eternally separated from God. But we are different! We are "looking for and hasting unto the coming of the day of God" because we "look for new heavens and a new Earth, wherein dwelleth righteousness." We are excited about the coming of the Lord, knowing that all things will be made new and perfect. Sin and Satan will no longer torment people. Instead, Jesus and the righteousness of God will prevail in Heaven and in Earth.

> **So, beloved, since you are expecting these things, be eager to be found by Him [at His coming] without spot or blemish and at peace [in serene confidence, free from fears and agitating passions and moral conflicts].**
>
> **2 Peter 3:14 AMP**

Because we have the security of knowing our eternal future, we can live our lives differently than those who do not know the Lord or His Word. Peter challenges us to be eager to please Jesus, so that when He comes back, He will find us living godly lives in peace. Instead of being carried away by fear and doubt and sin, we will be strong and confident in our faith, free of all bondage.

Consider that the long-suffering of our Lord [His slowness in avenging wrongs and judging the world] is salvation (that which is conducive to the soul's safety), even as our beloved brother Paul also wrote to you according to the spiritual insight given him,

Speaking of this as he does in all of his letters. There are some things in those [epistles of Paul] that are difficult to understand, which the ignorant and unstable twist and misconstrue to their own utter destruction, just as [they distort and misinterpret] the rest of the Scriptures.

2 Peter 3:15-16 AMP

Peter tells us the reason Jesus is waiting as long as He can before He comes back. He wants to get as many people saved as possible! Our main objective, until He comes, is to lead as many to the Lord as we can, planting the Word into people's hearts wherever we go. Our eternal perspective keeps our primary objective in the forefront of our lives, which is the Great Commission Jesus gave us in Mark 16:15, before He ascended to the Father. We are to preach the Gospel and make disciples of all nations.

Then in verse 16 of 2 Peter 3, Peter begins to talk about the Word of God and specifically Paul's writings. He says, "Look, some of Paul's stuff is hard to understand, and that's why those who aren't dedicated to the Word of God twist it and pervert it to get their own way. They don't allow the Word to rule their lives, so they end up in a mess."

Let me warn you therefore, beloved, that knowing these things beforehand, you should be on your guard, lest you be carried away by the error of lawless and wicked [persons and] fall from your own [present] firm condition [your own steadfastness of mind].

But grow in grace (undeserved favor, spiritual strength) and recognition and knowledge and understanding of our Lord and Savior Jesus Christ (the Messiah). To Him [be] glory (honor, majesty, and splendor) both now and to the day of eternity. Amen (so be it)!

2 Peter 3:17-18 AMP

The last words Peter wrote to the church were a warning to stick with God's Word, to not bend it and manipulate it to please ourselves, but to mold our lives to the unadulterated truth, to grow in grace and true understanding.

To be eternally-minded, don't change the Word of God; let the Word of God change you! Be diligent to study the Bible and allow the Holy Spirit to show you what God is saying to you. Don't be like those who refuse to accept what He says in His Word because it requires them to change, so they decide to change His Word to accommodate their selfishness. That is doing the opposite of having a spiritual makeover!

Remaining steadfast in God's Word gives you an eternal perspective that is not caught up in the things of this world, things that will soon pass away and that can put you off balance. Most important, living your life from an eternal perspective will always bring glory and honor to Jesus.

Refresh Today's Priorities

His mercies are new every morning!

Have an eternal perspective and be at peace by studying God's Word no matter what is going on in your life today. If you don't know how to study, ask your pastor or Sunday school teacher. They will be overjoyed to show you how to use concordances, commentaries, lexicons, and all the wonderful study tools that are available to you. Then, as you study, let the Holy Spirit—not your personal opinions, agendas, or feelings—be your guide. Throw open your heart to Him and allow Him to change your heart and mind with His Word.

Day 4

FORMULATED FOR TRUSTING CHRIST

We should be to the praise of his glory, who first trusted in Christ.

Ephesians 1:12

When the apostle Paul wrote this in the unction of the Holy Spirit, he wrote, "who *first* trusted in Christ." He was not praising God that he had trusted in Christ second, third, fifth or last. He was thanking God that he *first* trusted in Christ. Why did he make this point? Trusting in Christ above all else will cause you to live a life of balance and meaning. People will testify of the difference you made in their lives. Your friends and family will speak of the great impact you have on them because you never take your eyes off Jesus and you trust first in Him at all times.

Getting saved is more than having all your sins forgiven and going to Heaven. Salvation is not living like the world and forgetting about God until you get ready to die. Being saved is belonging to Jesus, forever. Your life is His and His life is yours. It means that instead of looking to other people and things to save you in your everyday problems, you trust Jesus first.

You cannot fully trust anyone but Christ. You can't trust this world. The news media is frequently biased so you can't trust them. People who don't know or follow the Lord are usually thinking only of themselves and what they want. Even ministers of the Gospel are still contending with their flesh and can fail you. How many Believers have turned their backs on God because, instead of trusting first in Christ, they trusted in a TV preacher who fell? Other Christians can compromise, get weighed down with hidden sins and cares, and refuse to surrender certain areas of their lives to the Lord. So, it is important that your bottom-line trust is in Christ and Christ alone.

To live a life that means something and pleases God, you must choose to trust Him before you get out of bed in the morning and throughout your entire day. No matter what hard times you face or desperate situations you find yourself in, you choose to trust Him to see you through to victory. You seek first His counsel and let the Holy Spirit and the Word direct your path.

In 1 Timothy 5, Paul talks about how wives and widows should conduct themselves. In verses 11 and 12 he rebukes the young widows who have turned to worldly pursuits instead of putting God first. The language he uses is extremely strong. He says, "Having damnation, because they have cast off their first faith." Damnation is experiencing the opposite of God's love and blessing. In practical, everyday terms, it means that when you trust in anything or anyone but Jesus, you *dam up*, block and hinder His blessings and favor from manifesting in your life.

It is hard for Jesus to reveal His love for you and bless you when you don't trust Him first. The widows' first faith was faith in Jesus to save them from their sins and from Hell. Once they were assured of their eternal salvation, however, they turned to the world's ways of living. This dammed up the blessings of God and He was unable to bless them. Their lives must have gotten pretty miserable!

As pastors, we too often watch men and women get caught up in the world and begin to fellowship with and even date people who are not saved. There is nothing wrong with having fellowship with unbelievers—as long as you trust in Christ first and keep Him number one in your life. Then you will influence them to also make Christ first in their lives. However, when you begin to confide in and lean on unbelievers or become romantically involved with an unbeliever, you are making them a greater priority than Jesus. Believers who live this way have constant turmoil and sadness in their lives because they leave their first faith in Christ to put their faith in the things of this world. They settle for a life that is far below what God has for them and nearly always end up compromising their beliefs and their moral standards.

When you put God first and trust in Him, you won't have to compromise your beliefs or moral standards to have friends, find a mate or live a valuable and happy life. When you live a balanced godly life, you will draw others to you who also do the same. You will also attract people who desire to live a godly life. Then, when your life on Earth is over, you'll have a sense of peace because you *first* trusted Christ.

REFRESH TODAY'S PRIORITIES

His mercies are new every morning!

Today ask the Holy Spirit to reveal any hypocrisy or self-deception, pride or arrogance, where you really trust more in yourself or someone or something else than you trust in Christ. Decide that in every moment of today and the days to come, Jesus is the first person you will look to for help and comfort. He is your best friend and wisest counselor. When you set this simple priority, to trust Him first, you will find yourself living a life that means something.

Day 5

HUMILITY BY DESIGN

Whosoever therefore shall humble himself as this little child, the same is greatest in the kingdom of heaven.

Matthew 18:4

I don't want to just get by in the Kingdom of God; I want to be great! Don't you? Jesus told us that if we desire to be great we must humble ourselves like little children are humble. When you stop to think about this, little children are completely dependent upon their mother and father. They see the world around them through their parents' eyes, and everything they learn about life comes from their parents. They love their parents unconditionally. They trust their parents implicitly. They are open and completely honest—sometimes to the parents' embarrassment!

As long as children follow the example and instructions of their parents, they live a balanced, happy life. The minute they rebel or follow worldly strangers, thinking they know better, they get into trouble. In Matthew 23:12, Jesus gave us this instruction and warning, "Whosoever shall exalt himself shall be abased; and he that shall humble himself shall be exalted." If we want to be great in the Kingdom of God, this is really important information! We cannot go around promoting ourselves; we must let God promote us. Someone said once, "If you promote yourself, then you will have to keep yourself there; but if God promotes you, He will keep you."

Of all the apostles, Peter was probably the worst at trying to promote himself. When Jesus said that someone would betray him, Peter cried, "If I have to die with You, I will not deny You!" (Mark 14:31 NKJV). Then later, of course, he denied Jesus three times, and the Bible says he wept bitterly. This same Peter later wrote,

Humble yourselves therefore under the mighty hand of God, that he may exalt you in due time:

1 Peter 5:6

After Jesus was resurrected, one of the first things He did was show Peter that He was forgiven for denying Him. (See John 21:15-17.) Jesus said to him three times, "Do you love Me?" and each time Peter answered, "Yes, Lord. You know I love You." And each time Peter answered Him, Jesus said, "Then feed My lambs. Feed My sheep." He was telling Peter, "Okay. You're forgiven. Now go do what I've called you to do!"

By this time, Peter was a lot more humble than he had been at the Last Supper! Because he humbled himself under

Jesus, God used him in a powerful way. In Acts, chapter 2, when the disciples were baptized in the Holy Ghost and began speaking in tongues, Peter is the one God chose to deliver the first evangelistic sermon. Peter was the first preacher in the Church! God exalted him because he had humbled himself.

One thing Peter knew for certain: if we don't humble ourselves, God will humble us! He loves us too much to see us walk around in pride and self-righteousness, causing all kinds of trouble for ourselves and the people in our lives. When Peter preached his second sermon, just after he and John had healed the crippled man at the Gate Beautiful, he taught what he had lived through. He told us how we can get rid of pride and humble ourselves.

Repent ye therefore, and be converted!

Act 3:19

We don't have to wallow around on the floor, crying, "Oh, Lord Jesus! I'm such a worm! How can You ever forgive me? My life is over!"

No! All we have to do is repent. No drama. No big scene. We just say, "I repent, Lord. I take my medicine and I make the adjustments in my life. Thank You for Your grace and mercy. Thank You for forgiving me and cleansing me from all unrighteousness according to 1 John 1:9. I humble myself under Your mighty hand, love and guidance."

Repent simply means to change our minds, our posture, our position, our attitude. We turn our lives around. While we were sinning we were walking in the wrong direction, but then we repented by doing a one-eighty so we could walk with Jesus in the right direction. At the same time, we also need to be *converted.* It took humility to repent and change our ways and direction, but it also takes humility to allow the Holy Spirit to convert our hearts to where they need to be. We need to be like children, completely dependent upon God for every breath we breathe and every step we take. Our eyes must be on Him and our ears tuned to His Spirit and His Word at all times.

Humility is more than just a good, submissive attitude. Humility is also love in action. Jesus was our perfect example.

Let this mind be in you, which was also in Christ Jesus:

Who, being in the form of God, thought it not robbery to be equal with God:

But made himself of no reputation, and took upon him the form of a servant, and was made in the likeness of men:

And being found in fashion as a man, he humbled himself, and became obedient unto death, even the death of the cross.

Philippians 2:5-8

Jesus made Himself of no reputation. Although He was God, He chose to become a servant to all human beings by submitting to a cruel death on the cross, paying the debt for our sin and bearing all of our punishment. He was the greatest

Servant, and that is why His name is exalted above every other name.

> **Wherefore God also hath highly exalted him, and given him a name which is above every name:**
>
> **That at the name of Jesus every knee should bow, of things in heaven, and things in earth, and things under the earth;**
>
> **And that every tongue should confess that Jesus Christ is Lord, to the glory of God the Father.**
>
> **Philippians 2:9-11**

After the Word of God shows us how Jesus humbled Himself, the Holy Spirit goes on to exhort all Believers to follow His example.

> **Wherefore, my beloved, as ye have always obeyed, not as in my presence only, but now much more in my absence, work out your own salvation with fear and trembling.**
>
> **For it is God which worketh in you both to will and to do of his good pleasure.**
>
> **Philippians 2:12-13**

When we humble ourselves, we are bringing our salvation, the power of God, from the inside to the outside of our lives. We are allowing the saving grace of Jesus Christ to flow out of our spirits and direct our minds, our conversation and our actions. This is how God is pleased with us! Our humility toward Him gives Him the opportunity to grow us up and move us out so that His good pleasure is accomplished.

I want you to notice that verse 13 says, "not as in my presence only," which means we are to be humble no matter where we are, who we are with or what we are doing. Humility is simply living for God instead of living for ourselves. He is the only One we are trying to impress!

Refresh Today's Priorities

His mercies are new every morning!

Who are the people in your life you want to impress? All children want to please and impress their parents, and when we grow up we still want to please them—no matter how good they were as parents. We want to impress our friends, our family members, our boss and co-workers and our neighbors. That's why we need to repent and be converted! To be humble as a little child, we need to love and serve—not impress. As we humble ourselves under the hand of God, loving and serving others, then we will be great in His Kingdom. Be great today by being humble.

Day 6

A Fresh Look at Your Inheritance

Blessed be the God and Father of our Lord Jesus Christ...

In whom also we have obtained an inheritance, being predestinated according to the purpose of him who worketh all things after the counsel of his own will:

That we should be to the praise of his glory, who first trusted in Christ.

Ephesians 1:3,11-12

When we are born again we obtained an inheritance; and that inheritance is for a purpose. We are to use our inheritance to do the will of God and bring glory to Him. The apostle Peter tells us in 2 Peter 1:3 that "His divine power hath given unto us all things that pertain unto life and godliness," which means everything we need to live a holy, powerful and joyful life was ours the moment we were saved. Now that is an awesome inheritance!

As we examine our priorities, the question always comes up: "Where does money fit into all this?" If any area in our lives needs balance, it is probably our finances! Obviously, we need money to live our lives, and God's Word says that He has already provided everything we need, so that must include money. But the Bible also gives us a strong warning that we need to be very careful what our attitude is toward money.

The love of money is the root of all evil: which while some coveted after, they have erred from the faith, and pierced themselves through with many sorrows.

1 Timothy 6:10

None of us want to live like this! We don't want to err from the faith or to be pierced with many sorrows, so we must guard our hearts and minds to have the right perspective on money. The Word does not say that money is evil; it is the *love* of money—coveting it, letting it motivate everything we do, getting satisfaction and security from it, and obsessing over it—which is the attitude that leads to all evil.

Money and materialism go together. We can look at our checkbook ledger or our credit card bills and tell a lot about what our priorities are. How do our tithes, offerings, and charitable donations compare with money spent at department stores, grocery stores, fast-food restaurants, movies and other entertainment? Now please don't go telling everyone that I said you shouldn't dress nice, have fun and go out to dinner from time to time! My purpose here is just to challenge you to look at how you are spending your money to determine more about what your real priorities are.

One of the things I don't want to do is put you in bondage by telling you how much time you need to spend or how much money you should spend on the various needs and activities of your life. Each of us has a unique life to live in Jesus Christ, and my schedule and where I spend my money may be different from your schedule and the way you spend your money. For example, if you are a fashion designer, you may spend a lot more money on clothes than I would because it is your calling and you want to be excellent in presenting yourself in a fashionable way. The Word of God is telling us that our inheritance is for a purpose, and your purpose will cause you to use your inheritance in a different way than I will use my inheritance.

What I do want to do is encourage you to put God first in everything, and that includes money. You won't love money if you love God more than anyone or anything else. Loving Him is the key to keeping the right motive and perspective toward every area of your life, especially money. When you go before Him throughout your day, He will give you the wisdom you need to spend your money wisely. In this way you will be a good steward of all He's given you in your inheritance in Jesus Christ, and you will glorify Him with it.

When I stand before Jesus to give account of my life, I don't think He's going to be interested in hearing excuses and explanations. I can't say, "Well, Lord, You know, I had children, and these kids just took so much of my time. I was married to Creflo, and he was running all over the world, and I was trying to keep up with him. Then I had this fear that I never really could get over. I just really didn't have time to figure out where I was spending money and how I was using my inheritance. I'm sorry, Lord." None of that is going to fly with Him! No, I want to stand before Him knowing I used the inheritance He gave me—the inheritance He bought and paid for with His life and blood—to do His will and glorify His name throughout the Earth.

Everybody wants to get something for nothing, but it's going to cost us some time, money and energy to get on the course God has for us *and stay there*. I think we do somewhat of an injustice by telling people, "Just give God your heart and everything will be all right." Certainly, receiving Jesus is the best decision anyone can make, and He will change your life for the better in an astounding way. However, when Jesus preached the Gospel, He didn't cut any corners. He made sure people understood the commitment they would be making to live for Him, especially when it came to money.

Then said Jesus unto his disciples, If any man will come after me, let him deny himself, and take up his cross, and follow me.

For whosoever will save his life shall lose it: and whosoever will lose his life for my sake shall find it.

What is a man profited, if he shall gain the whole world, and lose his own soul? or what shall a man give in exchange for his soul?

Matthew 16:24-26

Are you trying to make a deal with God or have you given Him your whole heart and life with no strings attached? He gave His life for you and saved you just the way you are. Now He asks for you to give your life to Him and accept Him fully as your Lord. By fully trusting Him with your whole life, He promises you will find it; but if you hold back anything from Him, you will lose it. And one of the areas we have a hard time giving completely to Him is money and material things.

The Bible is very relevant to this day and time in which we live. Our westernized, modern minds often think it is outdated or hard to understand because it was written so long ago, but people are people. Human beings are the same in any time, place and situation. And Jesus is the same yesterday, today, and forever! (See Hebrews 13:8.) When He spoke to the rich young ruler, He was also speaking to many of us.

Jesus said unto him, If thou wilt be perfect, go and sell that thou hast, and give to the poor, and thou shalt have treasure in heaven: and come and follow me.

But when the young man heard that saying, he went away sorrowful: for he had great possessions.

Matthew 19:21-22

Like many people today, this young man did not want to give up his money and possessions to follow Jesus. Some Christians are just as unwilling. They do not want Jesus to be Lord of their money and all the things they own because they are afraid He will ask them to give it all away. However, they will lose their own soul when they hold on to what is really His in the first place! Everything we have comes from Him and is for His use and pleasure. (See Colossians 1:16.)

Now look at how the disciples reacted to what happened with the rich young ruler.

Then said Jesus unto his disciples, Verily I say unto you, That a rich man shall hardly enter into the kingdom of heaven.

And again I say unto you, It is easier for a camel to go through the eye of a needle, than for a rich man to enter into the kingdom of God.

When his disciples heard it, they were exceedingly amazed, saying, Who then can be saved?

But Jesus beheld them, and said unto them, With men this is impossible; but with God all things are possible.

Matthew 19:23-26

The disciples also must have had some money or they would not have been so alarmed, saying, "Who then can be saved?" Even they struggled with money getting control of their hearts and putting them out of balance! As always, Jesus gave them the answer: "But with God all things are possible." If we stick with God and love Him and serve Him before money, possessions, or anything else in our lives; He will help us keep our hearts right, use our inheritance wisely and give all the glory to Him.

REFRESH TODAY'S PRIORITIES

His mercies are new every morning!

When you are paid, do you consider that money to be yours or the Lord's? Do you just give Him ten percent and an offering or two, or do you consider all of it to be His? The next time money comes into your hand, whether it is a gift or a paycheck, ask Him to show you the purposes for that money. I think you will be surprised! He wants you to pay your bills and bless those who have served you with electricity, a home and food. He wants you to give generously to your church and those in need. He also wants to meet your needs in abundance and bless you in special ways. So today, look at all you possess as His. Use your inheritance for His purposes and His glory!

Day 7

Anti-Idolizing

We know that we are of God, and the whole world lieth in wickedness.

And we know that the Son of God is come, and hath given us an understanding, that we may know him that is true, and we are in him that is true, even in his Son Jesus Christ. This is the true God, and eternal life.

Little children, keep yourselves from idols. Amen.

1 John 5:19-21

The apostle John ended his first epistle with these words, maybe because the Holy Spirit wanted that last verse to remain ringing in our ears as we lived our daily lives. "Little children, keep yourselves from idols." Worshipping idols is not just buying a statue of some pagan god and bowing down to it every day. Worshipping idols can be much more subtle. It is giving our devotion to anything but God.

In verse 19, the Holy Spirit tells us that the whole world lies in wickedness, and there are plenty of things and people who can distract us from walking in an attitude of worship toward God or pull us away from God. Then one day we wake up and realize that our hearts and minds are consumed with a certain relationship or activity that has replaced God by becoming our first priority. That is idolatry.

Idolatry will put your life completely off balance because you are focused on the wrong thing. When you give your attention to something that is unstable, always changing position, and untruthful, your life will begin to reflect those negative attributes. To be balanced, you must keep your eyes on Jesus. You cannot love anyone or anything more than Him.

My husband and I have a wonderful relationship and marriage. I love, respect, and admire him. However, he is not my God. If my devotion to him overshadowed or replaced my devotion to God, I would be worshipping a false god. Idolatry is worshipping and being devoted to false gods. The only true God is the God of the Bible, the Father of Jesus Christ.

When you worship someone or something, you make them the first priority and final authority in your life. If watching sports is your idol, then you set your priorities and arrange your life around sports. The moment you get off work all you can think about is getting home and turning on ESPN, getting to the baseball field to watch your favorite team play, or coaching your son or daughter's soccer team. There is nothing wrong with any of these things unless they have taken over your life and become an idol, taking the place of God in your life. If God is truly your God, then He is always the first thing on your mind and the One who always has your whole heart. You set your priorities and arrange your life by His Word and the leading of His Spirit. It's really just that simple.

I've said this before, but it bears repeating. Going to church a couple of times a week is not giving God first priority in your life. You cannot go to church and worship God with a passion, live like the world the rest of the time, and keep yourself from worshipping idols. If you think and speak and live like the world, you will be devoted to the things the world is devoted to. The world loves and is devoted to a lot of things that can distract you from God and even oppose God. That's why we are warned again and again to guard our hearts and minds from the world.

To keep yourself from idols, you must keep your heart and mind from being captured by anything and anyone other than Jesus Christ. He must always be your first love. You can love other people. You can enjoy all kinds of activities. You can even spend time with unbelievers and work in the world. You can do all this if Jesus remains your first love and none of these other people or things grab your heart the way He does.

You may profess that God is your first priority on Sunday, but is that profession reflected in your lifestyle on Monday? Do you wake up and throw a fit if your wife doesn't have the coffee made? Do you walk into your office and snap at those under your authority but act all courteous and compliant to your boss? If you are doing these things or anything like them, you are probably spending more time with other interests than you are with God. Just going to church on Sunday will not cut it! It is an illusion to think that you are following Christ unless you are manifesting His love and walking in the Spirit at home and at work—not just at church.

In 1 John 2:15 it says, "Love not the world, neither the things that are in the world. If any man love the world, the love of the Father is not in him." I have never heard anyone on their deathbed talk about their car, their newspaper, or their office and say, "Just let me see it one more time!" That is because the things of this world are not eternal, and they do not matter in light of the eternal life and love we have in Jesus. If we are completely wrapped up in the love of God, we will not get tangled up in and idolize the things of this world.

The world will never satisfy the deep longings and needs of our souls. We can climb the corporate ladder to success, and the world may make a big fuss over us, but it never fulfills us. It is never what we thought it would be. And how much did we have to compromise or lose in order to get there? I used to think that it took money to do everything. It doesn't take money. A day of God's favor will put you light years ahead of what it takes others a lifetime of struggle to obtain.

When we put God first we will keep ourselves from idols, and everything else will be in order. Our family will be in order, and we won't have to neglect them and compromise our beliefs to be successful. God wants us to keep ourselves from idols because He has the best plan, the best way, and the greatest blessings to give us.

First John 5:20 says that Jesus came and gave us an understanding of these things "that we may know him that is true, and we are in him that is true." This is a powerful statement! We literally abide and live and operate in Him who is true. Therefore, we can discern the lies of the enemy, the deceptions and distractions of the world, and anything else that would try to draw us away from God and bring us into the bondage of idolatry. Being in Jesus we can live like Jesus, who was in the world but not of the world, because we have His understanding.

REFRESH TODAY'S PRIORITIES

His mercies are new every morning!

Be honest with yourself today. Who or what has captured your heart? What do you think about and spend your energy on more than anything else? If there is anything or anyone else who gets more of your attention than Jesus, it's time to back away from it or them. Then acknowledge Jesus in everything you think, say and do, instead of just crying out to Him whenever you need help. Keep yourself from idols by being His partner in life.

Day 8

CLEAN FROM THE LOVE OF THE LORD

Love not the world, neither the things that are in the world. If any man love the world, the love of the Father is not in him.

For all that is in the world, the lust of the flesh, and the lust of the eyes, and the pride of life, is not of the Father, but is of the world.

And the world passeth away, and the lust thereof: but he that doeth the will of God abideth for ever.

1 John 2:15-17

Just in case you have any doubts about how devastating and destructive it is to love the world and live like the world, I am going to show you from God's Word how foolish, unsafe and imbalanced it is. For example, if I allowed the world to direct my path as a mother, I could follow books and "experts" that advise everything from never disciplining my kids to ruling them with an iron hand. I would be in total confusion as to what was right. Moreover, since the world's ideas are based on fear and not faith, I would probably raise my kids in a lot of fear.

First John 2:15-17 above says that if I don't love the world or adopt its ideas and attitudes, and I just do the will of God, what I will produce will abide forever. My children will have eternal life. That sounds a lot better than the world's way! That's why I tell my children, "You want me to get before God!" They know that if I put God first, spend time with Him, and commune with Him all day, I will have the love, wisdom, patience and courage to do what is right for them. I will be effective and productive as their mother and love them in the right way.

If I stay away from God and get caught up in my kids' schedules, suddenly I am just a taxi service who's running them here and there, at my wit's end, and no good to anybody. I have no peace. I have no joy. Instead of meditating on God's Word, my mind is filled with distractions and problems. Consequently, I have no answers! I have no wisdom or patience to deal with all the little foxes that are nipping away at me through my children. They are just trying to grow up, and they need me to be strong in God so I can help them sort out their lives according to the Word of God and teach them to follow the Spirit for themselves.

The first example our children have is us. If we live our lives with God as our first priority, then it is almost certain they will, too. By putting God first in our lives, we not only have the grace to be good parents, also we help to insure that our kids will walk in that same grace when they are adults and have children of their own. "Train up a child in the way he should go: and when he is old, he will not depart from it" (Proverbs 22:6). The training up of a child is done mostly by example. In the end, your children are going to imitate what you actually said and did more than what you told them to say and do.

Raising children is just one area of life that flourishes when we refuse to love the world or follow its ways and instead abide in God's Word. If we are a godly example in the way we live our lives, loving God and not loving this world, the world takes notice! The unbelievers around us will be touched by our compassion and challenged by our wisdom. They will be struck by the favor of God on our lives. They will see the difference God makes and want to turn from doing things the world's way to doing things God's way. Most of all, they will want to know God like we know God.

It's not hard to see that the world is going to Hell in a handbasket! If we love it and put our trust in it, our lives will crumble as it crumbles because lust fulfilled leads to death and destruction.

You are jealous and covet [what others have] and your desires go unfulfilled; [so] you become murderers. [To hate is to murder as far as your hearts are concerned.] You burn with envy and anger and are not able to obtain [the gratification, the contentment, and the happiness that you seek], so you fight and war. You do not have, because you do not ask.

[Or] you do ask [God for them] and yet fail to receive, because you ask with wrong purpose and evil, selfish motives.

Your intention is [when you get what you desire] to spend it in sensual pleasures.

You [are like] unfaithful wives [having illicit love affairs with the world and breaking your marriage vow to God]! Do you not know that being the world's friend is being God's enemy? So whoever chooses to be a friend of the world takes his stand as an enemy of God.

James 4:2-4 AMP

When God ceases to be your first love, you become your first love! All you want to do is please yourself and experience pleasure. Your first priority is to gratify your flesh, and nothing fully satisfies. This leads you to hate, to jealousy and envy, to anger and rage, to strife and war with others because you always want more and are never fulfilled. What's worse, you commit spiritual adultery and act like God's enemy, as Adam did when he sinned against God in the Garden. He was the first person to love the world more than God.

Thank God, what Jesus did on Calvary is far greater than what Adam did in the Garden of Eden! By God's grace given to us in Jesus Christ, we can overcome the lusts of this world and not fulfill the lusts of our flesh. If God's grace was sufficient for Paul to overcome his thorn in the flesh, His grace can enable us to defeat the lusts of our flesh, the enticements of the world and love only Him. How do I know this? Because God's Word says in Acts 10:34 that He is no respecter of persons, that He is faithful to perform His Word for anyone who puts their trust in Him and only Him.

There is a lot at stake here! God has placed a destiny in your heart, and the enemy and the world will do anything they can to talk you out of it or take it and use it for evil. The world is not your friend! And if you try to be the world's friend or do things the world's way, you will be robbed of your divine destiny. The only way to avoid this heartbreak is to put God first at all times and in all situations. You must trust Him, His Word and follow His Spirit over what the world says or does. He is the only One who can take you where you really want to go!

REFRESH TODAY'S PRIORITIES

His mercies are new every morning!

Today the Holy Spirit is calling you to break off any love affair with anything outside the Kingdom of God and be willing to be different! Don't be ashamed of being called "Miss Goody-Goody" or "Mr. Holier Than Thou" because Jesus' priorities are your priorities. He was also talked about, misunderstood and persecuted. In the end, the world will perish and Jesus will be the acknowledged King of the Universe! And because you choose to love not the world and love and serve Him, He will see to it that you succeed in your divine destiny, just as He did.

Day 9

WASHED AND WITHOUT
BLEMISH

Wherefore, my beloved, as ye have always obeyed, not as in my presence only, but now much more in my absence, work out your own salvation with fear and trembling.

Philippians 2:12

This verse of Scripture is very powerful and life-changing when we understand what it is saying. Paul is not only telling the Philippians to obey the Word and walk in the Spirit whether or not he is with them, he is also telling them to work out their salvation with fear and trembling. Doesn't sound like a very pleasant time, does it? If you just read this verse without studying it in light of the rest of the Scriptures, it sounds like being saved is a frightening experience! But that isn't what Paul is talking about here.

When he says "work out," Paul literally means to bring the spiritual reality of being a child of God that is on the inside of us to the outside of us, to our soul and body. We let it be evident to all around us that we belong to Jesus. And sometimes, in order to do that, our soul and our flesh are going to go through some fear and trembling because they have not been completely converted and made perfect and whole yet.

Our minds, emotions, wills, and bodies are in the process of being brought under submission to the Holy Spirit in our spirits. The Holy Spirit is literally bringing a godly balance to our entire being: spirit, soul and body. What is pure and right and true may not seem like it to our souls and bodies at first. So, there is a process of maturity that every Believer goes through which involves some fear and trembling in order to begin to think and behave like Jesus.

I'm sure you have won people to the Lord, or you have brought them to the church and they were saved, and you saw the Lord touch them. Maybe they were healed or delivered from demons as well. It was obvious that something supernatural happened and they were changed in that moment. You encouraged them to go to church to be fed the Word of God and fellowship with the saints so they could continue to grow in their walk with the Lord. Yet, for some reason they just couldn't seem to get there. Then one day you met them on the street somewhere and noticed they were a little bit nervous around you. They just wanted to get away from you as fast as possible.

Instinctively you know that for some reason they weren't able to be consistent in all the things you do every day, like reading your Bible, praying and entering into praise and worship. And you know they haven't been attending church. This happens with so many, and I dare to say it is because their old nature, the sin nature, pulls them back into their old ways of thinking and doing things. The sin nature has succeeded in getting them off balance. They aren't unbelievers or bad people. It is not that they don't love the Lord. Their unrenewed minds prevent them from living from the inside out. They are falling back into living from their carnal desires and thinking, instead of living from their spirits.

Wherefore lay apart all filthiness and superfluity of naughtiness, and receive with meekness the engrafted word, which is able to save your souls.

James 1:21

The Amplified Bible says, "So get rid of all uncleanness and the rampant outgrowth of wickedness, and in a humble (gentle, modest) spirit receive and welcome the Word which implanted and rooted [in your hearts] contains the power to save your souls." The Word of God, planted and rooted—not just heard and forgotten—is where we get the strength and ability to live from the inside out!

The moment a person is saved, they can avoid a lot of heartache and trouble if they understand and accept the priority to renew their mind with the Word of God. When we talk about renewing the mind, what are we really talking about?

That he [Jesus] **might sanctify and cleanse it** [the church] **with the washing of water by the word,**

That he might present it to himself a glorious church, not having spot, or wrinkle, or any such thing; but that it should be holy and without blemish.

Ephesians 5:26-27 [brackets mine]

When we read and study the Bible, the Living Word (Jesus) washes our minds. He washes away all the lies and filth and "superfluity of naughtiness" we have picked up from living in the world. He drives out all these devices of the enemy with His powerful truth. Submitting ourselves and aligning our lives with God's Word is like taking a bath in His supernatural power and holiness; and when that happens for the first time, we understand what it means to be *renewed!* It's almost like getting saved all over again.

When we are new in the Kingdom of God, sometimes we don't realize that just like we have to wash ourselves in the natural every day with soap and water, or we begin to stink, we also have to wash ourselves in the Spirit and the Word every day. If we don't, our thinking, and consequently our behavior and decisions, will begin to stink! We have to dedicate ourselves to the process of bringing the love and truth on the inside of us to the outside of us by taking those daily baths in God's Word.

We smell great and are healthier by having a bath in the natural. Likewise, our thinking is more stable, our behavior more godly, and our lives more pleasant when we spend time renewing or cleansing our minds in God's Word every day.

Holiness cannot always be determined by someone's actions because we are holy and belong to God the moment we are born again. But a person can be saved spiritually and outwardly yet act like the devil from time to time. As I said before, there is a process in learning to live from the inside out, and that process takes time. If we aren't careful, we can look down on other Believers who are struggling through this process, thinking we're so much more diligent and have it all together.

Over the years, there have been things I was trying to get away from—bad habits, destructive thoughts and behaviors, and cravings for things that weren't good for me. I would try to stop doing what I knew was wrong on the outside, yet on the inside part of me—the sin nature that still resided in my flesh—I wanted to do it. I got really frustrated because my mind was not renewed to the point where I could make any permanent changes on the outside.

Sometimes it took a time of praying and crying out to God to just *want* to quit doing what I was doing! With some weaknesses and sins, we have to start by asking God to give us the desire to stop. We pray for this and water that prayer with the Word and pray in the Spirit to build our faith for our deliverance. That's the way the Word converts our souls and sets them right with God. Then, when all desire for that sin is gone, it is much easier to appropriate His strength and wisdom on the inside of us and get rid of that thing we are doing on the outside.

This is walking inside out!

We no longer think like the world because we think from our spirits, from the person we are eternally, on the inside of us. Our heavenly Father created and designed us to live a balanced life. A priority in our Christian lives is not to be led by our bodies or our souls. We are to be led by the Holy Spirit in our born-again spirits—walking inside out.

Refresh Today's Priorities

His mercies are new every morning!

Today, be very conscious of the fact that the Holy Spirit lives *inside* you and will speak to you there. On the other hand, the enemy introduces thoughts and speaks to us from the outside. Do not be persuaded by other people to do things that give you no peace inside. If your spirit is crying, "Don't do that!" then don't do it! If you don't have peace on the inside, you cannot act in faith. Decide that today you will do all and say all in total confidence in the Lord by making it a priority to live from the inside out.

Day 10

Examine Yourself and Be Renewed

Examine yourselves, whether ye be in the faith; prove your own selves....

2 Corinthians 13:5

We are to examine ourselves regularly to make sure we are walking in the faith. If we are in the faith of God, trusting Him and His Word to provide for us in everything that concerns us, then we can live in peace and really produce something for His Kingdom. Being in the faith means living a Christlike life and following Jesus in all things. In this way, we live a balanced life.

One of the clearest ways to determine whether we are in the faith is to look at our priorities. Is Jesus still our first love? If He is, He will show up in every area of our lives. There are three ways we can tell what our priorities are: how we spend our time, what we talk about and what we think about.

How do you spend your time? What do you find yourself doing when you are not working or taking care of your family?

Are you laid up in front of the television all evening long, all day long? Are you at the mall shopping for stuff you don't need? Are you chatting on the Internet or playing video games for hours at a time? How about sports? Are you obsessed with football, basketball, baseball, soccer—or all of them?

There's nothing wrong with any of these activities as long as your time with the Lord comes first. You have to set the priority of having time with Him. Don't wait to find the time, because it won't happen. The angels are not going to come down, snatch the remote control out of your hand and put your Bible in your face! You're going to have to set your alarm clock to get up in the morning and pray. Then allow the Lord to speak. Don't be in such a hurry to get out and do what you want to do. He always has the best plan for your day and your life—and the answers to every problem you face. However, you have to take the time to listen if you want to hear from Him.

The second way we can discover our priorities is by paying attention to what we talk about most. I remember when I was working for a big company before I worked for our ministry. Everybody would complain, "I hate this job," "These policies are bad," "My boss is a jerk," and "I can't wait till I get home." Then they would go home and probably complain to their families.

I remember thinking, *All this complaining is not going to change the situation.* It reminded me of the children of Israel, who did a lot of whining and complaining and wandered in the desert for forty years. Their first priority was not God and His Word, and ultimately they did not go into the Promised Land. The truth we learn from their situation is that the only reason we whine and complain is because we don't believe and trust God. We don't think He will keep His Word, and we don't think He is great enough and loves us enough to defeat the giants who are keeping us from taking our Promised Land. Hebrews 3:7-12 warns us against unbelief, which is evil and often comes out of our mouths in complaining.

Jesus told us in Matthew 12:34 and Luke 6:45 that what we speak comes right out of our hearts. And in Mark 11:23-24, He taught us that what we believe in our hearts and speak with our mouths determine our lives. This is a spiritual law that applies to all human beings, saved or unsaved. We should make certain that what we are saying lines up with God's Word because, as His children, we know that we will have what we say!

If Jesus is your first priority in life, then your conversation with others will reflect that. I'm not saying to always quote chapter and verse, but Colossians 4:6 NKJV, says it best, "Let your speech always be with grace, seasoned with salt, that you may know how you ought to answer each one." We should always be speaking in line with the truth of God's Word, planting seeds of truth with grace into every life we touch. This eliminates gossip! If we are always talking about other people and their business, then we are not walking in the grace and love of God, and He is not our first priority.

The third way we can tell our priorities is what we think about. What do we meditate on when our minds are not occupied with family, work or ministry? Psalm 1:2-3 says that if we meditate on the Word of God day and night, we will be blessed and successful in every area of our lives. The battle of good and evil is won between our ears! What we think about most is going to determine whether Jesus is Lord or the devil has his way with us.

In this battle our only offensive weapon is the sword of the Spirit, which is the Word of God. (See Ephesians 6:12-17.) The Bible tells us to continually renew our minds with God's Word so that whenever we face temptation, persecution, tragedy or some other attack of the enemy, we will stand strong in faith. When God and His Word are our first priority, we have His strength and wisdom to win every battle we fight.

It is so easy to let our minds wander all over the place. We can go anywhere in our own heads! We can go shopping. We can travel the world. We can indulge in romantic fantasies. God gave each of us an incredible gift when He created us with an imagination. However, we must use it and our mental capacities in a godly way if we want to have a life worth living. A mind that is always occupied to one degree or another with the Word of God and the things of God is going to be clear-thinking, reasonable and peaceful. As a result, what comes out of our mouths, the decisions we make and our behavior will bring great prosperity and success.

All three of these things—time, talk and thought—reveal our priorities and bring either balance or imbalance to our lives. They are also interrelated. How we spend our time affects what we think, and what we think determines what we speak. When we spend a lot of time on something, we will think and talk about it a lot. Likewise, what we think and talk about a lot is what we will spend our time doing. Time, talk and thought work in harmony, and one will affect the others. That's why our time, talk, and thought should always be ruled by God and His Word.

Refresh Today's Priorities

His mercies are new every morning!

You are probably tired and worn out at the end of your day, but give Jesus the last few minutes. Read a few verses of His Word, turn out the light, and pray in the Spirit as you drift off to sleep. Give Him a moment to speak to you. He wants to be involved in every part of your life. He wants to comfort you and direct you. He wants to prepare you for tomorrow so you can walk in all His blessings and favor. Then you will awake refreshed and ready to face every challenge, knowing He is with you all the way.

Day 11

MAXIMIZE YOUR TIME

I trusted in thee, O LORD: I said, Thou art my God.

My times are in thy hand.

Psalm 31:14-15

Our times are in God's hand. Therefore, in order for us to stay balanced our time should be spent as He directs us. How we spend our time is a real indication of our priorities. We like to judge ourselves by our good intentions and then judge other people by their actions. However, if we really want to bring a godly, radical change into our lives, we must judge *ourselves* by our actions. When we take an honest look at what we are doing with our time, and particularly look at what we are doing in our "free" time, we will see what our priorities truly are.

Time isn't always going to be as it is now, and we have to live with that in mind. The older I get, the more I live each day as if it might be the last day before Jesus comes back. What is most important to me today, then? I want to walk in the love of God, kiss my husband, hug my children, and be doing what

God wants me to be doing from moment to moment. As I minister, I minister as if it's the last opportunity for me to minister before Jesus returns. When I live like this, I am seeing things from God's eternal perspective instead of the world's temporal perspective.

The world doesn't really care that there is a God to whom one day they will have to give an account for how they lived their lives. We, as children of God, know we have been predestined to be conformed to the image of Jesus (Romans 8:29), and that we have a divine calling to fulfill. This makes our time very important, and it is not something we should ever take for granted. Time is a very precious thing in the eyes of God.

Blessed is he that readeth, and they that hear the words of this prophecy, and keep those things which are written therein: for the time is at hand.

Revelation 1:3

You are blessed by reading the Word, however, you are even more blessed by *keeping* the Word of God. You don't just hear a message or read the Bible and continue living your life as before, doing whatever you want to do. You change your life to conform to the Word of God. Why is this so important? The time is at hand! This is something that is written several times in the New Testament.

And he saith unto me, Seal not the sayings of the prophecy of this book: for the time is at hand.

Revelation 22:10

You are spending your time right now! Your time is your most valuable asset, and in most instances your time is more valuable than money. That is why you must be careful to spend it the best way, carrying out God's will and purpose for your life. We are also reminded throughout the Word of God that our time on Earth is short, so we want to make the most of it.

When things are brought to a crisis throughout the Earth, we can sense that the period of fulfillment of God's Word is near. Jesus said in Matthew 24:6-7 that there would be an escalation of wars, earthquakes, famines, and all kinds of terrible catastrophes on the Earth just before He comes back. Are we not seeing these things happen today? Every believer with any knowledge of biblical prophecy senses that the time is short before the return of the Lord, Jesus Christ.

The devil also knows that his time is short, and he is taking every opportunity he can to keep people from believing and living the Word of God. He is the source of imbalance! He knows that not only does the quality of our lives depend upon how we spend our time, so does the will of God being carried out in the Earth. The impact we have for God on this world is dependent upon how we spend our minutes, our hours, our days and our years. We cannot let the enemy stop us from making the most of our time for Jesus!

One of the ways we can make the most of our time is to manage it. Instead of walking aimlessly through life, we can have a plan. In Habakkuk 2:2 it says that we should write down the vision so that others may read it and run with it. God never calls anyone to accomplish something alone. We are members of a Body, and some of those members may be waiting for you to write a vision from God so they can read it and run with it! Even if you are the only one involved for the time being, the best way to keep Satan from stealing your time is to write the vision and make it plain. Outline everything in as much detail as possible so that you can plan your days around your priorities. Believe me, if you don't plan your days, the enemy will plan them for you!

The greatest amount of your time—actually all of your time—should be spent with the Lord. I know you are thinking, *How can that be possible? I can hardly make time to read my Bible and pray as it is!* It is really very simple. You continue to have that special time where it is just you and God—when you pray, study His Word and listen to His voice. Then you do other things *with Him* instead of on your own. You are continuously in His presence, so you might as well include Him in everything you do. By acknowledging Him at all times and in all situations, He is truly your first priority, and we have seen that when He is your first priority, everything else falls into place. You won't waste any time and Satan cannot steal any time if you are continuously walking with the Lord.

I find a lot of Christians who are content with just having fire insurance—just escaping Hell—and they never really experience victory like they could. They believe their time on Earth belongs to them. They forgot that time comes out of God and is for His purposes. All things were created by Him and for Him, and that includes time. We must always remember that our times are in His hand.

Refresh Today's Priorities

His mercies are new every morning!

Are you living your life for yourself or for God? You can tell by looking at how you spend your time. Are you in a continuous conversation with the Lord all day long? If not, try it for an hour. Try it for half a day. Try it for a day. And then try it for the rest of your life! Your time will become His time, your life will become His life, and no matter when Jesus comes, you will be ready!

Day 12

SEASONS IN LIFE

Hearken unto me, O Jacob and Israel, my called; I am he; I am the first, I also am the last.

Mine hand also hath laid the foundation of the earth, and my right hand hath spanned the heavens: when I call unto them, they stand up together.

Isaiah 48:12-13

Meditating on scriptures like these will keep us from getting so full of ourselves! The Word always keeps us balanced. The Holy Spirit reminds us that we didn't call the Earth into being. The Earth doesn't spin by our knowledge and our intellectualism. We didn't determine the boundaries of the water or fling the stars into the heavens. Everything we are and have is from God, and He alone knows the times and seasons of our lives.

Time was created by God, and when time is no more, God will still be here. Before God set time into motion, before this Earth was created, before man was created, God was here. After all that is said and done and time stops, God will still be here. We do ourselves an injustice when we don't live in the context of how God sees time. He views our lives in *His* understanding of time.

God alone knows how each moment should be spent, and He gives us a lot of instruction about that in His Word.

> **Come ye near unto me, hear ye this; I have not spoken in secret from the beginning; from the time that it was, there am I: and now the Lord GOD, and his Spirit, hath sent me.**
>
> **Thus saith the LORD, thy Redeemer, the Holy One of Israel; I am the LORD thy God which teacheth thee to profit, which leadeth thee by the way that thou shouldest go.**
>
> **Isaiah 48:16-17**

From the beginning God has been speaking to us through His prophets, and the book of Hebrews tells us that now He speaks to us through His Son, Jesus. (See Hebrews 1:1-2.) He has put His own Spirit inside us so that we can hear Him at all times. Sometimes He will tell us about our future. Through His Word and His Spirit, mostly He desires to tell us what we should do from moment to moment.

We must begin to see that time comes out of God and is a God-given opportunity. Time is not a means to live unto ourselves but to live like Jesus—unto God.

> **So, since Christ suffered in the flesh for us, for you, arm yourselves with the same thought and purpose [patiently to suffer rather than fail to please God]. For whoever has**

suffered in the flesh [having the mind of Christ] is done with [intentional] sin [has stopped pleasing himself and the world, and pleases God],

So that he can no longer spend the rest of his natural life living by [his] human appetites and desires, but [he lives] for what God wills.

1 Peter 4:1-2 AMP

Jesus is always our perfect example, and He spent every second of His time on Earth living for "what God wills" instead of living "by [his] human appetites and desires." Because He lived this way, He fulfilled everything prophesied about Him in the Old Testament for that period of His life on Earth. He fully satisfied the Father.

The way we use our time determines whether we count for God and please Him. Therefore, by pleasing Him, we do His will. I think sometimes we forget about simple things like this. We take tomorrow for granted. We take next week for granted. We take time for granted, yet God says always to be conscious of the fact that time is short and precious in this hour.

Teach us to number our days, that we may apply our hearts unto wisdom.

Psalm 90:12

Even the psalmist needed help with how he spent his time! He is asking God to help him number his days, just like we are now. Numbering our days is a very serious thing. It means we weigh our days and judge our time by how we love and serve God. We hold ourselves accountable for the hours we spend each day. Like Jesus, we are careful with our time. We use it to move in the direction God has pointed us to go and to accomplish what He has instructed us to accomplish.

I read a story of a man who worked long hours in business, sacrificing time with his family in order to get ahead and to be noticed, until one day everyone wanted to hire him. He had all the job offers he had ever dreamed of having. He told his wife, "We've arrived!"

Her response was, "Yeah, but at the wrong place."

Her simple statement got his attention. He had accomplished his goal to succeed in business, but he was losing his family. This brief conversation with his wife began a transformation of his goals, and he said to her, "Maybe we should prioritize our life and everything we do on the basis of who we want to see crying at our funeral." His life turned around, and changing his priorities saved his marriage and his family. If he had continued working only to see himself established and wealthy in business, he may have lost his wife and children and lived a miserable life. He would have lost what was most important to him because he was not viewing his time through God's eyes.

All of us have to make sure we don't live our lives working for things that have little to no lasting value. We must remember God and time. When our lives are over, we are not going to arrive in Heaven and look for our stock portfolio. We are not going to ask where the nearest sports arena is located. We are going to walk through those pearly gates to see Jesus! Then we will look for all the lives we touched and those who touched us in His name. Seeing our time here on Earth through God's eyes, in light of eternity, is one of the things that helps us keep our priorities straight and our lives in heavenly balance.

REFRESH TODAY'S PRIORITIES

His mercies are new every morning!

How are you managing your day today? How are you using your time? Are you "spending" it or are you giving it to God? Sometimes we just need to change the way we view something, to see it as God sees it, in order to change our lives for the better. Take this simple idea of giving your time to God instead of spending it on yourself. Let Him decide how you will spend each moment and see what happens.

Day 13

WORSHIP AND REPLENISH

Now there were in the church that was at Antioch certain prophets and teachers; as Barnabas, and Simeon that was called Niger, and Lucius of Cyrene, and Manaen, which had been brought up with Herod the tetrarch, and Saul.

As they ministered to the Lord, **and fasted, the Holy Ghost said, Separate me Barnabas and Saul for the work whereunto I have called them.**

Acts 13:1-2 (italics mine)

In this passage of Scripture, the Holy Spirit gives us a picture of the saints at Antioch. We can see that He spoke clearly to them when they ministered to the Lord. All of us want to hear clearly from the Lord so that we can stay in His will and keep our lives balanced and holy, so ministering to the Lord is very important. The truth is, when Jesus is our first priority, we will continually minister to Him. But what does that mean in practical terms? What exactly is ministering to the Lord? Is it fasting, as is mentioned in verse 2? Is it praying? Is it giving food and clothing to the poor? Is it doing what He's called us to do in our profession and ministry?

Recently, I began to understand more about what ministering to the Lord really is. I would hear Creflo sing around the house and realize that he was ministering to the Lord in a very simple, easygoing way. Looking at these verses of Scripture in Acts, chapter 13, I saw that part of what the saints at Antioch were doing was singing to Him. It didn't matter whether they had great voices or were on the praise team. They just got before God by singing to Him. They put themselves in a position to receive from Him by lifting up their voices in praise and worship.

Ministering to the Lord puts you in a position to receive whatever He wants to give you. In this case, Paul and Barnabas received their ordination and commission to preach the Gospel, and the rest of the saints received two apostles. These apostolic gifts were given to both the Body and to the world, gifts that would be powerfully used by God to minister to Believers and unbelievers throughout the known world. Therefore, we should never underestimate the importance of ministering to the Lord! At any time, the Holy Spirit may speak something powerful that will change and transform us and the world around us.

There are some things the Holy Spirit wants to say to us, and do in and through us, but He cannot say or do anything unless we take the time to minister to Him. I could not hear the voice of the Spirit by just watching my husband minister to Him as he sang around the house. I had to begin to minister to the Lord myself. Paul exhorted us to speak to ourselves "in psalms and hymns and spiritual songs, singing and making melody in your heart to the Lord" (Ephesians 5:19). He painted a great picture of what should be going on in our lives whether we are with other Believers or by ourselves.

When singers with beautiful voices get up in church to sing, we all really enjoy it; but who are they ministering to? When we sing our praise and worship songs, are we just enjoying the wonderful music or are we ministering those songs to the Lord? Praise and worship becomes a dead ritual and a spiritually dull recital when the saints do not minister to the Lord with their whole hearts. It is great to minister to one another with music, but if we aren't first ministering to the Lord, eventually there will be no ministry to the people, either.

Hast thou not known? hast thou not heard, that the everlasting God, the Lord, the Creator of the ends of the earth, fainteth not, neither is weary? there is no searching of his understanding.

He giveth power to the faint; and to them that have no might he increaseth strength.

Even the youths shall faint and be weary, and the young men shall utterly fall:

But they that wait upon the Lord shall renew their strength; they shall mount up with wings as eagles; they shall run, and not be weary; and they shall walk, and not faint.

Isaiah 40:28-31

This is one of the most famous and powerful passages of Scripture about the blessings that come from ministering to the Lord. We thank God that He never faints or grows weary, that His understanding of all things—of us especially!—is unlimited, and that He gives us His power and strength to go on when we are mentally, emotionally and physically drained.

Verse 30 then speaks of a time when even the young people will faint and fall, but verse 31 says that those who "wait upon the Lord" will be strong as eagles, run without getting tired and walk without feeling weak. Hallelujah! I want to be one of those eagles who are always ministering to the Lord, don't you?

Obviously, those who make it a priority to minister to the Lord will do great exploits for the Kingdom of God. These saints have spent enough time with Him to know that He never gets physically tired or fed up with them, and He has unlimited wisdom to meet any situation they face. They know whatever they desire and need comes from Him, He loves them, and He is their sole source of strength.

When you get faint and weary, that is the time to rejoice and minister to the Lord because He wants to give you His power. He gives power to the faint! When you run out of might, He gives you strength to go on. And when you have no earthly idea what to do about your situation, He has the answer. There are times when you need more than a pat on the back and an encouraging word. You need God's instructions on how to handle tricky situations and His strength to carry out those instructions.

Isaiah 40:31 in *The Amplified Bible* says, "Those who wait for the Lord [who expect, look for, and hope in Him] shall change and renew their strength and power; they shall lift their wings and mount up [close to God] as eagles [mount up to the sun]; they shall run and not be weary, they shall walk and not faint or become tired." Ministering to the Lord draws us close to Him, where we receive His strength and wisdom, and He prepares us to run!

REFRESH TODAY'S PRIORITIES

His mercies are new every morning!

Take the time to minister to the Lord and wait upon Him, and expect Him to speak to you. He's an ever-present help in the time of trouble, always there, longing to commune with you and give you answers and insight. Sing to Him. Let Him know what He means to you. Tell him your whole heart, and then He will tell you His!

Day 14

A Tranquil Soul

Do not fret or have any anxiety about anything, but in every circumstance and in everything, by prayer and petition (definite requests), with thanksgiving, continue to make your wants known to God.

And God's peace [shall be yours, that tranquil state of a soul assured of its salvation through Christ, and so fearing nothing from God and being content with its earthly lot of whatever sort that is, that peace] which transcends all understanding shall garrison and mount guard over your hearts and minds in Christ Jesus.

Philippians 4:6-7 AMP

How many days do you wake up and your first thought is, *O God, how am I going to make it?* In the past I spent a lot of my time and energy worrying about all kinds of things, and scriptures like these convicted me and I had to stop. When God said, "Don't fret or have any anxiety about anything," He meant everything! Why? Because whether it is just a little tension or a huge phobia, fear in any form keeps you off balance and miserable.

Back then I tried to imagine being so peaceful all the time that nothing would bother me or cause me to be anxious or nervous. My question was, "How, Lord? I know nothing is impossible to You, and You wouldn't tell me to do something if it wasn't possible, but this really seems impossible! You know how terrifying this world can be. Have You read the news, lately?"

In verse 6, God doesn't just tell us not to fret. He also gives us something to do to defeat fear, worry and anxiety. We are supposed to pray, tell Him what we need, and do it with an attitude of thanksgiving. Now, we cannot be thankful if we don't expect something to be thankful for! That's why we make our requests to God in faith, knowing He loves us, will protect us, and already has a solution to our problems.

The next verse talks about the power of our salvation. Do you know what the power of our salvation is? It is God's love. He revealed His love for us when Jesus died for our sins on the cross. Now, we can pray to Him without being afraid of Him. He breathed His Spirit into us and gave us a new spirit and a new life. We not only have the desire and the power to overcome temptation, but He sat us right next to Him with Jesus and gave us His authority over all the power of the enemy. All these things make up the power of our salvation, so we have no reason to fret!

People who don't make their relationship with God their first priority never know His love for them and the power of their salvation. As a result, they are always fretting and tend to continue to be afraid of Him in a bad way. We are to fear Him in the sense of reverence and awe; however, we are never to be afraid of Him because we are His beloved, precious children. And when we see the greatness of our salvation, which is revealed in His Word, our faith soars, fear flees, and peace guards our hearts and minds.

We need to be assured of who we are and what we have in Jesus Christ. Then we can put our worries to rest and walk in His wholeness—nothing missing and nothing broken—in spirit, soul and body. This peace is so amazing that we can never understand it, but we can live in it and enjoy it!

Continuing in this passage in the book of Philippians, the apostle Paul tells us some other things we need to do in order to stop fretting.

> **Finally, brethren, whatsoever things are true, whatsoever things are honest, whatsoever things are just, whatsoever things are pure, whatsoever things are lovely, whatsoever things are of good report; if there be any virtue, and if there be any praise, think on these things.**
>
> **Those things, which ye have both learned, and received, and heard, and seen in me, do: and the God of peace shall be with you.**
>
> **Philippians 4:8-9**

Whatever is true, honest, just, pure, lovely, of a good report; whatever is filled with virtue and praise of our God—

these are the things we are to meditate on if we want His peace to continually flood our souls and drive out all worry and fear. Very simply, if Jesus is our first love and number one in our lives, verse 8 describes what we will think about.

Then comes the doing. Paul says, "You've learned a lot of godly things from me. You've learned by watching my example, by hearing me preach and teach God's Word, and by spending time with me. Now go out and do these things yourself. Live a balanced, productive life in front of others." You can't just hear something, know about it and succeed. You must also appropriate it, do it and make it a part of your life.

Refresh Today's Priorities

His mercies are new every morning!

On a sheet of paper, make a list of everything that makes you fretful, worried, afraid, anxious, tense, or nervous. Then on another sheet of paper, make a list of what is true, honest, just, pure, lovely, of a good report, virtuous, or praiseworthy in your life that cancels out what you put on your "fret list." The assurance of your salvation is that it is so great, so powerful, that nothing can stand against it. The Word of God and the Holy Spirit in you can make your fret list melt away and disappear—forever!

A Richer Life Through Prayer

He Himself existed before all things, and in Him all things consist (cohere, are held together).

Colossians 1:17 AMP

Jesus existed before anything else existed. He existed before the Earth was created, before you were born, before your wife or husband came along, before your children were conceived, before your job or your ministry manifested—before any part of your life or anything that concerns you. Jesus existed before and therefore comes before. He is the first priority in your life.

Colossians 1:17 also says that in Jesus Christ all things are held together—ALL things. He holds the universe together. He holds the Earth together. And He holds every atomic particle together in perfect balance. Scientists have always marveled that every solid object we see is mostly air, and they have spent a lot of time trying to figure out just what holds things together. The Bible gives them the answer: Jesus!

In Him, ALL things consist and are held together, and that includes your marriage, your family, your ministry, your business, your job, your health, your wealth, and your general well-being. If your life is flying apart and falling to pieces, it is probably because Jesus is not before all things in your life. Look around you and observe the lives of those who do not put Jesus first, who do not recognize that His hand holds their lives together. Their lives will be chaotic and confusing, too. Of all people in this Earth, Believers should have the most happy, productive lives. They should have it all together. But even we won't have it all together if we don't allow Jesus to put us together and keep us together!

He also is the Head of [His] body, the church; seeing He is the Beginning, the Firstborn from among the dead, so that He alone in everything and in every respect might occupy the chief place [stand first and be preeminent].

Colossians 1:18 AMP

It really doesn't get any clearer than this! Jesus is the Head of His Body, the Church, of which we are members. He is my Head and your Head, our Leader and King. He occupies the chief place by Himself, and He is first and preeminent—the most important person in our lives. Because of all this, we should be talking with Him more than anyone else, and talking to Him is what the Bible calls prayer. When Jesus is before all things in your life, you are in a continuous attitude of prayer.

Prayer enables you to know God—Father, Son and Holy Spirit—and to receive from Him all that you need to become the person He has destined you to become and fulfill His call on your life. Prayer is where your victories happen. In your personal time with Him, you get direction for your life, you get wisdom and strength to keep going, and sometimes you get chastised and cleaned up inside!

I'm talking about your personal, private prayer life. Corporate prayer and listening to messages on prayer are great things; however, without your own private prayer life, your relationship with God will suffer, He will not be your first priority, and then you will suffer. Prayer is more important than having a ministry, running a business or raising a family because none of these things are going to be successful without prayer. I'm not saying that these other things do not have an important part of your life; I'm saying they must be built on the foundation of your prayer life in Jesus Christ.

Prayer is not just setting aside a certain time each day to speak in tongues and make your requests known to God. That is great; however, it is only the beginning because prayer is communication with Him. He lives in you and you live in Him, so you can talk to Him anywhere, at any time.

When I spend the day with my family, I talk with them and enjoy their presence during the whole day. When one of my children wants to talk to me about something, I don't say,

"Not now. It's not our family time." And the same holds true for prayer. I just enjoy God's presence and have a running conversation with Him throughout my day, no matter what I'm doing.

There have been many times when God has stopped me in my tracks and cautioned me when I was about to do something I thought was a good idea. To my natural mind everything looked fine, but He knew something I didn't know. Later, I would see why He had stopped me. If He had not been before all things in my life at that moment, and I had not been in an attitude of prayer to hear Him, I would have made a big mistake.

Prayer is also not a formal, religious thing. You don't have to talk to God in King James' English, saying, "I thank Thee, O Lord, for the bounty that Thou hast given." He knows how you talk! He hears you talk to your family and friends. He knows how you talk to yourself. In fact, He knows more about you than you do! So you best drop the religious jargon and just get real with Him.

There are lots of prayer groups today, and intercessory prayer has become a big thing in the church. This is good because it reveals the priority and importance of prayer; however, it can be detrimental to living a life of prayer. Some Believers go to prayer meetings; passionately pray long, Word-filled prayers; and never pray until the next prayer meeting. Then they wonder why their lives are in turmoil. It's because Jesus really doesn't come before anything else in their lives, so they are talking to Him only when they are with other Believers.

We need to make certain that our lifestyle reflects what we say we believe. If Jesus is before all things in our lives, then we will be in an attitude of prayer throughout our day, always communing with Him, living a life of balance. The world will see the difference He makes because He will hold our lives together when the world around us is in pieces.

Refresh Today's Priorities

His mercies are new every morning!

Today, you cannot hold your life together! Only Jesus can do that, which is why you must put Him before all things. If you haven't already done it, establish a private time of prayer each day. Then continue to talk with Him and enjoy His presence for the rest of your day. Your life will become richer and fuller if you determine in your heart to do what the Word of God commands you to do in 1 Thessalonians 5:17, "Pray without ceasing." That means, talk to Jesus at all times!

Day 16

PERFECT PEACE

Peace I leave with you, my peace I give unto you: not as the world giveth, give I unto you. Let not your heart be troubled, neither let it be afraid.

John 14:27

Jesus gave us a key to always having our priorities straight and living a balanced life in this verse of Scripture. We are always quoting Philippians 4:7, "And the peace of God, which passeth all understanding, shall keep your hearts and minds through Christ Jesus," but do we really understand that this is extraordinary peace because it is the peace of Jesus? When He was resurrected and ascended to Heaven, He gave us an incredible gift: *His peace.*

Examining our priorities from day to day can be either a pain in the neck or a joy, depending on whether we are walking in peace. If we are immersed in the peace of Jesus, we can look at our lives honestly, transparently before God and make whatever adjustments we have to make to prioritize and achieve balance. One of the things I have begun to realize is that we tend to think we are more spiritual than we really are.

Sometimes we allow deception to come in simply because we are quick to judge other people and fail to judge ourselves. And one of the most important questions we need to ask ourselves regularly is, "Am I walking in the peace Jesus gave me?"

Before Jesus left the Earth and gave us His peace, He talked a lot about it. He told us that we should not worry about anything, that there was no anxiety in the Kingdom of God.

> **Therefore I say unto you, Take no thought for your life, what ye shall eat, or what ye shall drink; nor yet for your body, what ye shall put on. Is not the life more than meat, and the body than raiment?**
>
> **Behold the fowls of the air: for they sow not, neither do they reap, nor gather into barns; yet your heavenly Father feedeth them. Are ye not much better than they?**
>
> **Which of you by taking thought can add one cubit unto his stature?**
>
> **And why take ye thought for raiment? Consider the lilies of the field, how they grow; they toil not, neither do they spin:**
>
> **And yet I say unto you, That even Solomon in all his glory was not arrayed like one of these.**
>
> **Wherefore, if God so clothe the grass of the field, which to day is, and to morrow is cast into the oven, shall he not much more clothe you, O ye of little faith?**
>
> **Matthew 6:25-30**

Jesus was a human being, and He knows what we humans are concerned about. If we don't eat and drink, we will die. If we don't have the proper clothing, we could get sick and die. We have essential needs, and for many of us it is a daily struggle to see that these needs are met. Jesus tells us not to take thought about these things. We are literally never to think about where our next meal is coming from or what we will wear tomorrow!

The birds and the flowers are examples in nature of living things God cares for, and we know He cares for us much, much more. So we are not to sit around biting our nails over these matters. In verse 27 He says our worrying cannot change anything. Worry is just another manifestation of fear, fear destroys faith, and without faith in God and His Word, nothing good is going to happen in our lives.

Jesus gave us His peace so we could always walk in faith. If we go back to John 14:27, we read that Jesus gave us peace and a command to go with it: "Let not your heart be troubled, neither let it be afraid." We cannot maintain peace if we allow our hearts to be troubled by anything. Our hearts can be troubled by fear, worry, doubt, unbelief, anger, frustration, jealousy, greed, pride—just about anything that is the opposite of the character and nature of God—and all these things come to us in the course of our daily lives.

Fear is one of the worst enemies of our faith. It is important that we don't allow our lives to be conducted by fear. This is a big challenge in this world of terrorism, all kinds of natural disasters, and talk that even the air we breathe is not safe. But if Jesus were here on Earth right now, He would not be afraid. He would be at peace, and we have His peace! Therefore, we can walk in this world in peace.

The moment our hearts become troubled in any way, we need to stop and allow the Holy Spirit to deal with that issue. If we notice we are nervous, anxious, angry, grieved, or discouraged, we need to ask why we are feeling that way and defeat it before it captures our minds. Fear and other enemies of peace can snatch the life of God from us and cloud our ability to make good decisions and have good judgment. But the peace of Jesus puts us in position to hear the voice of the Holy Spirit clearly and have faith and confidence in God's Word.

The Comforter, which is the Holy Ghost, whom the Father will send in my name, he shall teach you all things, and bring all things to your remembrance, whatsoever I have said unto you.

Peace I leave with you, my peace I give unto you: not as the world giveth, give I unto you. Let not your heart be troubled, neither let it be afraid.

John 14:26-27

There is a direct relationship between having the peace of Jesus and hearing the voice of the Holy Spirit, and because the Holy Spirit reveals God's Word to us, we must be able to hear Him at all times. God has given us that ability, and we don't want to do anything that would hinder us from hearing Him. We must keep our hearts in peace.

Now, I know it is impossible to keep from feeling any kind of negative emotion or having any bad thoughts. But as Brother Kenneth E. Hagin used to say, "You can't help the birds flying over your head, but you can keep them from making a nest in your hair." Feeling fear or anger is a common human experience, and having a jealous or doubtful thought happens from time to time; but you don't have to sit around and entertain them! The Bible tells us exactly how to keep our hearts from being troubled with them.

> **Though we walk in the flesh, we do not war after the flesh:**
> **(For the weapons of our warfare are not carnal, but mighty through God to the pulling down of strong holds;)**
> **Casting down imaginations, and every high thing that exalteth itself against the knowledge of God, and bringing into captivity every thought to the obedience of Christ.**
>
> **2 Corinthians 10:3-5**

We cannot live according to our carnal, human reasoning and walk in the peace of Jesus. We must cast down and throw out any thought that does not line up with what we know about our heavenly Father, our Lord and Savior Jesus Christ, and our Comforter and Teacher, the Holy Spirit. The poison that is trying to steal the peace of Jesus from us has an antidote: God's Word. Jesus said, "Be not afraid, only believe"

(Mark 5:36). When we believe the Word of God and meditate on His truth instead of churning in wicked imaginations, we get rid of that thing that is trying to trouble us and are restored to the peace of Jesus.

REFRESH TODAY'S PRIORITIES

His mercies are new every morning!

What is troubling you today? Maybe you are just nervous about something. Perhaps you are upset with someone who offended you. It might be that you looked in the mirror and saw some wrinkles, and the fact that you are growing older scares you! No matter what it is that is bothering you, you can defeat it by turning to God's Word and being restored to the peace of Jesus. Allow His peace to rule your heart and mind, and all your troubles will be resolved. Sound too simple? It is! We try to make it so complicated, and God always keeps it simple.

Day 17

FULFILLED BY THE FATHER

We have had fathers of our flesh which corrected us, and we gave them reverence: shall we not much rather be in subjection unto the Father of spirits, and live?

Hebrews 12:9

Even though God is the creator of the universe and the Most High, He is also your Father. The Word says He is the Father of spirits, and you are a spirit being. Who you really are is His spiritual child! As a spirit being, you will live forever; and as the spiritual child of God, you will live forever with Him in perfect balance and joy.

If you are going to spend eternity with someone, it is a good idea to get to know them. That's why the Bible tells us to "be in subjection unto the Father of spirits." The Word of God also says that by staying in subjection to our heavenly Father, we will live. In other words, we will appropriate His life into our lives. Getting to know our Creator is one of the greatest blessings He gives His children!

As you get to know the Father, you will soon find out that He is not a divine traffic cop who is just waiting for you to break the law so He can penalize you. That's what so many people, even Believers, think of Him. It is true that He is a holy God and His goodness will lead you to repentance if you do sin, and He does that because He loves you and wants you to be happy and succeed in life. You are the apple of His eye, the joy of His joy, the love of His love, and He longs to fellowship with you. He draws you close to Him so you can know Him better, and when you see how much He loves you, you are just going to want to hang around Him all the time! You are never going to want to get into sin again and separate yourself from Him.

Loving our fathers and wanting to hang out with them is the way God made us because He is a Father. He wanted sons and daughters to share His creation with Him. He created us for love, fellowship and pleasure. We should not compartmentalize Him into little segments of our lives; instead, we should allow Him to be a part of everything we do. On the golf course, at work and at home, He's there and we can talk to Him. We can consult Him on every matter.

I've just painted a really beautiful picture of fatherhood, yet we see very few natural fathers who come close to that picture. Even in the church many fathers today put their profession before anything else, and their families suffer from their neglect and lack of affection. On the other hand, we also have a lot of fathers who run out on their children through crime and prison, drugs, alcohol or women other than their wives. Some just leave. Today, we have fathers who molest their children or someone else's children. We hear about fathers who murder their families and then take their own lives. Some fathers refuse to work and support their families even if they are there. They just hang around the house, eat, drink and watch television. When their kids come home, they don't care what they do; and when their wives come home from work, they expect them to do all the cooking and cleaning. Good fathers are hard to find today, and the reason we see this is because a natural father cannot be what he was created to be without making it a priority to know the heavenly Father.

Mothers are not exempt either! Women in society are saying things and doing things I never would have thought of as a young girl growing up. Today they can be just as violent, abusive and destructive as any man ever was. That's why motherhood has also taken a big hit. Mothers are aborting their babies before they are born and murdering them after they are born. They do not care enough for their children to discipline and instruct them. That's why so many kids are running wild in the streets, getting hooked on drugs and alcohol, and having sex and babies when they are still babies. Some mothers just take off and run away like men have been doing. Why are they behaving like this? They do not know the

Father who created them. If they did, they would be so filled with His love that they could never hurt their children. (See 1 John 4:7-8.)

When the disciples asked Jesus how to pray, Jesus said, "Always begin with 'Our Father.'" (See Matthew 6:9.) When we pray, we pray to the Father. This can be hard for those who have had terrible natural fathers. If you are one who struggles with the concept of a loving heavenly Father, you may need to forgive your natural father and ask God to heal your heart. Ask Him to show you all the lies you have believed about Him and tear down that stronghold! Your spiritual life begins and lives through eternity with the Father, so it is important for you to see Him as He really is.

The more you see the Father as He is, the more you will trust Him. Over time, as you pray without ceasing and surrender every area of your life to Him, you will see how He not only saved you from Hell but also from the day-to-day pitfalls and dangers of this world. You will also find that you are begging less, speaking His Word in faith more, and don't mind it when He calls you on the carpet to deal with some sin in your life.

I was the youngest child and the apple of my natural daddy's eye. I took advantage of it, too! I would aggravate my brothers just because I knew my dad would jump on them if they fussed at me. I knew I could get away with things because

Daddy loved me so much. I was his "sugar lump." But my spiritual Daddy loves me more—and knows everything! One day He jerked the slack out of my prayer life. I'm sure He had a twinkle in His eye when He said to me, "You only want to spend a lot of time with Me because you want My anointing when you've got to preach." His love is so great that He told me the truth about myself so I would grow in the integrity of my heart.

Your heavenly Father will reveal your heart to you. He will show you your *self*—the good, the bad, and the ugly—and who He created you to be. I can't tell you these things. In fact, I will observe someone and think something about them that isn't true at all! Then one day, I hear their testimony and see that I had no idea who they were or what God had brought them through.

Only your Father knows who you really are, why you received the gifts and talents you have, and how you can live your life to the fullest. Your brothers and sisters in Christ can help you discover these things; however, only an intimate relationship with Him will make you truly happy and fulfilled.

Refresh Today's Priorities

His mercies are new every morning!

Take a good look at your relationship with your earthly father, and then read the following scriptures about your heavenly Father, especially if your earthly father was not so great: Matthew 6:8, John 10:27-30 and 14:9, Romans 8:15, 1 Corinthians 8:6, Ephesians 1:17, Hebrews 12:9, and James 1:17. It is also helpful to read through the New Testament and see how many times the word *Father* is mentioned by Jesus and the apostles. Whether you had a good earthly father, you now have a Father in Heaven who is amazing!

Day 18

SHAPED BY WORDS

Inasmuch then as we have a great High Priest Who has [already] ascended and passed through the heavens, Jesus the Son of God, let us hold fast our confession [of faith in Him].

Hebrews 4:14 AMP

Our confession has a lot to do with the priorities in our lives. Do we talk about our problems all the time or do we talk about how big God is? What we speak is what we are magnifying, amplifying, making big, and enlarging in our hearts and minds. Our words determine the balance we walk in. What we say is also affecting everyone who hears us. Words can dash a hope or lift depression. We live by our words, so what we confess and how we talk has to be a priority in our lives.

Specifically, are we holding fast to our confession of faith in Jesus Christ or are we holding on to fear and worry? Jesus has paid the debt for our sin, taken all our punishment for it on the cross, and defeated the devil for us. He has triumphed in every way over every enemy to our souls: the devil, the world and the flesh. Now He sits in the heavens at the right hand of the Father, interceding for us because He knows what it's like to live in this world.

> **We do not have a High Priest Who is unable to understand and sympathize and have a shared feeling with our weaknesses and infirmities and liability to the assaults of temptation, but One Who has been tempted in every respect as we are, yet without sinning.**
>
> **Hebrews 4:15 AMP**

It's not so hard to hold fast to my confession of faith in Jesus when I consider what He has done and continues to do for me. It blows my mind when I try to fathom His love. I can miss the mark yesterday, and today I've got a new day! He's not thinking about what I did yesterday, that I didn't do what I should have done or should have known better than to get myself into something. That's why I say at the end of each chapter, "His mercies are new every morning!" (See Lamentations 3:22-23.) Every day I can wake up and know He has forgiven me and my life is fresh and new. I have another chance to get it right.

Jesus is our Lord and Savior and King, and He is also our High Priest. We do not have some high priest who cannot understand and sympathize with our weaknesses and infirmities. We have Jesus, who was tempted and tried and tested in every way that we are—but didn't sin. That makes

Him the perfect example to follow. What is also wonderful is that even though He is perfect, He is also compassionate.

Let us then fearlessly and confidently and boldly draw near to the throne of grace (the throne of God's unmerited favor to us sinners), that we may receive mercy [for our failures] and find grace to help in good time for every need [appropriate help and well-timed help, coming just when we need it].

Hebrews 4:16 AMP

When we are mindful of how merciful God is, and how He is so moved by the things we go through, we can also remember that He wants to bear our burdens. We don't approach Him arrogantly but boldly, confidently, and without apprehension or shame. He doesn't see us coming and say, "Oh no! Here she comes again, her old hardheaded self. And what's he doing here again? Every time I look up they are begging for something. These people are getting on my nerves." God doesn't see us like that!

Read your Bible. God loves us. We are His beloved children. He is patient. He is goodness and kindness personified. Whenever we need Him—three o'clock in the afternoon or three o'clock in the morning—He's there waiting and wanting to take that burden from us and give us His wisdom and understanding about it. He doesn't give us an "I told you so" sermon because His throne is a throne of mercy and grace. Mercy says, "It's okay. I love you and forgive you, and tomorrow's a new day!" Then grace says, "Because of your faith in Jesus and since you are My child, here's some supernatural strength and wisdom to overcome this situation." Hallelujah!

What does all this do to our confession of faith?

At one time in our ministry, we were suddenly eight million dollars behind in our bills. We recognized some of the decisions we had made that had gotten us into that place and went to God to obtain mercy and grace in our time of need. We said, "Lord, You know what this is," and He said, "Don't worry about it. Don't focus on it. And don't try to conjure up some way to manipulate people or come up with some kind of plan. Let Me handle it."

What did we say after that? What was our confession of faith? "God is handling it. It is going to be okay." And I tell you, it was over before we knew it! His was well-timed help—just when we needed it. There's nothing too hard for the High Priest of our confession!

Somebody said once that mankind's extremities are God's opportunities. When it seems hopeless and you are ready to lock your door and never answer the phone again because everyone you owe is after you, when you are backed into a corner because your boss wants you to do something "slightly illegal," when you feel trapped in an unhappy marriage and your kids are embarrassing you—that's the opportunity to go to the High Priest of your confession and receive some mercy and grace! He will understand, He will forgive, He will cleanse you of all unrighteousness and shame, and He will give you the answers you need to overcome.

REFRESH TODAY'S PRIORITIES

His mercies are new every morning!

Are you facing an overwhelming situation today? In 1 Peter 5:7, the Holy Spirit commands you to cast every care on Him. He says, "Throw it at Me! Roll it over on Me." He wants to relieve you and free you of all worry and fear. You have a High Priest who will take your burdens and give you answers—without condemnation or anger. He understands and has only His mercy and grace for you. Go boldly into His throne room to give Him your troubles and receive what you need from Him right now.

Day 19

Transformed in Him

I am the true vine, and my Father is the husbandman.

Every branch in me that beareth not fruit he taketh away: and every branch that beareth fruit, he purgeth it, that it may bring forth more fruit.

John 15:1-2

Living a balanced life by setting priorities is all about bearing more fruit for the Kingdom. If we want to bear fruit for our Father, there will be a time of purging when He tells us it is time to cut away stuff that just wastes time. Suddenly we see it how God sees it, our viewpoint becomes His viewpoint, and we put away things in our lives that distract us and hinder us.

If you have ever pruned a tree or bush, you know that sometimes you have to cut off a dead branch. In spiritual terms, these are all the distractions and time-wasters that take us away from living with and for God. Then sometimes you have to cut off a branch that's alive but growing in the wrong direction. This might be a person in your life who is taking you off course, and you find yourself making them a priority. You admire them and want them to like you, and one day you realize you're not being who you really are because you're trying to please some other human. That's when the Father prunes you with His Word by reminding you that He is the One you should be pleasing.

Now ye are clean through the word which I have spoken unto you.

John 15:3

The Word of God is a priority because Jesus is the Living Word. God speaks directly and personally to us in the Bible, and when He has an issue with us, the Holy Spirit brings the Word to our remembrance. Using the Word of God, He prunes and cuts away dead things in our lives, which purifies and frees us so we can bear more fruit for Him. We usually think of the Word of God as the "sword of the Spirit" in Ephesians 6:17, the offensive weapon God gave us to take authority over the devil and overcome all his attacks on our lives and the lives of those we care about. However, the Word of God is a double-edged sword that cuts both ways. While defeating the enemy, it also has another great purpose, which is to cleanse us, purify and help us to continually abide in Jesus.

Abide in me, and I in you. As the branch cannot bear fruit of itself, except it abide in the vine; no more can ye, except ye abide in me.

I am the vine, ye are the branches: He that abideth in me, and I in him, the same bringeth forth much fruit: for without me ye can do nothing....

If ye abide in me, and my words abide in you, ye shall ask what ye will, and it shall be done unto you.

John 15:4-5, 7

We are created and commanded to be fruitful and multiply, however, God has set things up so that we cannot bear fruit unless we are connected to Him, abiding in Him. We must live and move and have our being in Him. (Acts 17:28.) Then His love and life and power can easily flow through us to produce fruit for His Kingdom.

He tells us to abide in Him, so it is our responsibility to spend time with Him and seek Him first in all things. If our priorities get out of whack, it is our fault, not His! That means we are not spending enough time in His Word. We need to immerse ourselves in God's Word because that is His language, where He reveals His thoughts, His ways and His personality. Then when we pray we won't pray aimless prayers that are contrary to His desires. We will pray according to His will. John 15:7 says that if we abide in Him and His Word abides in us, our prayers will be powerful and effective.

Herein is my Father glorified, that ye bear much fruit; so shall ye be my disciples.

John 15:8

The mark of true disciples of Jesus Christ is that the Father is glorified in their lives. Because they abide in Jesus and are in continual communion with Him, their faces glow and they carry a fragrance of life and love that stays with them throughout the day. Their prayer life is fruitful, impacting their lives and other people's lives, and that gives glory to the Father.

What happens when we don't abide in God's Word and walk in the Spirit, praying without ceasing? Shortly after we get up in the morning, little irritations begin to surface during breakfast, and then we find ourselves blowing our horns in traffic, ready to jump out of our cars and have a fight. By the time we get to work, we are in strife with our coworkers, and we take absolutely no joy in what we do. We are bound up and can bear no fruit. About this time, we remember Jesus and decide that abiding in the Word is a much better way to live!

Abiding in Jesus brings peace, serenity, tranquility, joy, and a deep sense of purpose. Praying and abiding in Him also causes us to make some changes in how we govern ourselves. It enables us to shake off offenses and forgive quickly. Traffic jams are simply more time spent with the Father! Difficult coworkers are opportunities for the fruit of the Spirit to manifest in our lives. And our work is all done joyfully as unto the Lord.

If we abide in Jesus all week, church becomes much more exciting! We bring what we have learned and experienced with

God into the fellowship of other Believers. We join together as brothers and sisters, His children, with fully-charged spirits. Somebody has a song. Another has a testimony. One of the saints gives a word of prophecy, and we are all plugged in to the Father's heart! Praise and worship is vibrant and alive, and it seems that our pastor preaches the best message we have ever heard. The Word of God pierces our hearts and transforms us. We are forever changed, and we leave the church freshly anointed to bear even more fruit for our Father.

Everything in our lives is charged with the life and love of God when we abide in Him.

REFRESH TODAY'S PRIORITIES

His mercies are new every morning!

Today, as you read this devotional, you might have thought, *My life isn't like this! I don't glow all day, and it's all I can do to control my temper. I love the Lord, but most of the time I feel like I'm spinning out of control.* We all go through this, so please don't be discouraged! Whenever you can—good times or bad—breathe deep and remember Jesus. Just keep making the decision to abide in Him, and every day will get a little bit better.

Day 20

THE GLORY OF WISDOM

Wisdom is the principal thing; therefore get wisdom: and with all thy getting get understanding.

Exalt her, and she shall promote thee: she shall bring thee to honour, when thou dost embrace her.

She shall give to thine head an ornament of grace: a crown of glory shall she deliver to thee.

Proverbs 4:7-9

Setting our priorities to live in balance takes the wisdom of God. Without His wisdom, we can spend our time in all kinds of pursuits that have no lasting benefit for us or anyone else in the light of eternity. That's why the Bible tells us that wisdom is the principal thing. Wisdom promotes us, makes us honorable, enables us to walk in God's grace, and ultimately presents us with a crown of glory. We should pursue His wisdom because it will give us understanding of Him, His will and His purpose for our lives.

Pastor Creflo says, "Wisdom is the ability to use knowledge." We all have a lot of knowledge in these last days. You cannot watch television or surf the Internet today and not accumulate a lot of facts and information. And most people today spend a lot of years in school learning all kinds of things. However, we have to know how to use all the knowledge we gain. That's wisdom.

Who is as the wise man? and who knoweth the interpretation of a thing? a man's wisdom maketh his face to shine, and the boldness of his face shall be changed.

Ecclesiastes 8:1

Wisdom is an amazing thing! When a person walks in the wisdom of God, God's glory shines from their face. The light and warmth of His presence just emanates from them to others. And verse 4 goes on to say, "Where the word of a king is, there is power: and who may say unto him, What doest thou?" Not only will the glory and goodness of God come forth from Believers who walk in His wisdom, because they know and speak His Word, no one will be able to question the power and authority of their words.

There is no power, authority, or dominion other than that which has been granted by Almighty God, and Jesus is the King of kings. When you speak the words of King Jesus and walk in God's wisdom, the power of the Holy Spirit is there to back you up. Ecclesiastes 10:10 AMP says, "If the ax is dull and the man does not whet the edge, he must put forth more strength; but wisdom helps him to succeed." Human strength and understanding will accomplish only so much; however, wisdom sharpens or supernaturally empowers our human efforts so we don't have to work so hard!

In simple terms, God's wisdom helps you use good judgment. He has given you enough time to do His will for your life. If He hadn't, He would not be just and righteous. He also has given you His Spirit and His Word to enable you to walk in His wisdom and succeed.

Don't allow the devil to make you think you are not smart enough to do the will of God. If you are born again and filled with God's Spirit, if you have a Bible to read and study, then you have everything you need to accomplish God's purpose for your life. With His wisdom working inside you, transforming you and directing you, you can fulfill your divine destiny.

We may think we don't have enough time in the day to do everything we think we need to do. The problem isn't that we don't have enough time. The problem is that we just don't appropriate the wisdom of God to make the best use of our time. The difference between those who powerfully impact their generation for Jesus Christ and those who don't comes down to whether they use their time wisely. Our daily decisions—wise or unwise—make the difference between living an average, mediocre life and a life that changes the lives of those around us for eternity.

Another thing to remember is, you cannot walk in God's wisdom and be selfish and materialistic. You must have His desires and will at heart instead of your own to live the abundant life Jesus died to give you. In 1 Kings 17:10-16, Elijah illustrated this to a woman who was caught in the midst of a famine and had just enough oil and meal to make one cake. She told Elijah that she was going to bake it, and then she and her son were going to eat it and die. What did Elijah say to her? He said, "Give the cake to me instead."

Now this woman probably went through a lot of emotions when Elijah "selfishly" asked for the last food she had. Most of us would have probably said, "Look, man of God, why don't you command it to rain or have God send manna from Heaven for us?" Knowing he was a man of God caused her to take her eyes off of her own distress and focus on saving his life. She decided to act wisely, and the wisdom of God is always motivated by love for God and for His people. Elijah knew that. While his asking for the last bit of food looked selfish, in reality he was offering her God's wisdom in answer to her problem. Because she submitted her will to God's wisdom, the power of God came on the scene and that little cruse of oil and barrel of meal lasted until the famine was over!

God's wisdom gives us the ability to use the time and resources He has given us in the best way we can. Furthermore, His wisdom makes our faces to shine, our hearts to sing, and our lives to prosper in every area. With His wisdom we can easily set our priorities and do the right thing at the right time. We can be in the right place at the right time—everything in balance. And we can see miracle-working power all around us.

REFRESH TODAY'S PRIORITIES

His mercies are new every morning!

You might be wondering, *How do I get God's wisdom?* Every book in the Bible contains the wisdom of God, but the book that is primarily dedicated to revealing His wisdom in all the situations we encounter in life is the book of Proverbs. Meditating on verses from Proverbs can revolutionize the way you think and make decisions. There are thirty-one chapters in Proverbs, so I suggest you take a month with thirty-one days and read a chapter a day, picking out a verse or two to meditate on during your day. Then let what you read and meditate on influence your decisions. See if by the end of the month you are walking in much more wisdom than ever before.

Day 21

Awake and Be Refreshed

Try to learn [in your experience] what is pleasing to the Lord [let your lives be constant proofs of what is most acceptable to Him].

Take no part in and have no fellowship with the fruitless deeds and enterprises of darkness, but instead [let your lives be so in contrast as to] expose and reprove and convict them.

Ephesians 5:10-11 AMP

The Bible tells us what pleases God, and He wants to be first in our lives and to have the best of everything in us. When we awake in the morning, our first thoughts should be of Him. We should not wait until the end of the day when we are so tired we can't think straight to finally say hello to Him! We should give Him our first and our best. If we begin communing with Him first thing when we are rested and have some sense, then the rest of the day will be a whole lot easier!

Some people are more alert at night. The sun goes down and they come alive. They would much rather spend that special time alone with the Lord before they go to sleep. The evening is their first and best time to spend with Him. Then, when they wake up in the morning, they jump out of bed ready to go because they have heard from the Lord the night before. This is their way of giving their first and best to Him.

No one can tell you how to set your schedule and what to do with your time. That is something you have to work out with the Lord. The main thing is that you do! The verses above talk of learning what the Lord likes and doing what He finds acceptable. We are not just to take care of our families, make money to support them, and stay busy. Our lives are supposed to mean something, and they will mean something if we give God our first and best.

Verse 10 in the *King James Version* says, "Proving what is acceptable unto the Lord." Every now and again we are a proof of what our God says is acceptable because our lifestyle says that God is first and we give Him our best. We live our lives separated from the unfruitful works of darkness and speak and act only according to God's Word as the Holy Spirit leads.

The effects of living for God on those around you can be miraculous. I remember when I worked at a business before I came to work at the ministry. I didn't go around toting my Bible, passing out tracts to everybody, and jumping on my desk to preach; but I didn't stand around gossiping and complaining either. I just spoke the truth in love when the Holy Spirit opened a door of opportunity and obeyed the Lord throughout my day.

I knew that job was not my final destination. I knew God had something better for me, and I was just passing through. I did my job with excellence regardless of the situation. My conduct proved what was acceptable to the Lord and reproved any unfruitful works of darkness that were going on in the lives of those around me. As a result I saw many come into the Kingdom of God. They said it was just based on me having a quiet and meek spirit. You cannot underestimate the impact of a life lived putting God first and giving Him your very best!

Some Christians think they have to be like the world and make friends with unbelievers on their terms to lead them to the Lord. They hang out in the break room talking trash like the world, thinking they are going to draw people in and then present Jesus to them. What they don't realize is, they presented Jesus to them the moment they walked in the door. How they look, what they talk about, their work ethics, and their attitude—all these things are either going to say, "Jesus is the most important person in my life and I give my best in everything I do because of Him," or "I'm just here to hang out and be just like ya'll."

It is a shame even to speak of those things which are done of them in secret.

But all things that are reproved are made manifest by the light: for whatsoever doth make manifest is light.

Ephesians 5:12-13

Jesus told us that we are the light of this world. All we have to do is let His light and love shine through us to affect those around us and draw them to Him. Then His light will take care of the rest. When you walk into a dark room in the middle of the night, you don't stand there reproving the darkness, talking about how terrible it is. No! All you do is turn on the light. The light reproves and removes the darkness.

When you put God first and give Him your best in all you do, you are literally turning on the lights for those who are caught in the unfruitful works of darkness. Unfortunately, these may not all be unbelievers. There are some Believers who are so caught up in what the world thinks, says, wears and believes that they look like an unbeliever. They appear to be spiritually dead.

Wherefore he saith, Awake thou that sleepest, and arise from the dead, and Christ shall give thee light.

Ephesians 5:14

If you were lying in a hospital in a coma, you would look just like a dead person. No one could tell the difference between you, who were actually alive, and the rest who were dead. This is a picture of Believers who are living for themselves and by the world's standards instead of for Jesus. They are asleep among the spiritually dead! The Holy Spirit often sends us to these prodigal sons and daughters just to shine the light of God's love and truth on them. Hopefully, they will come to themselves and return to their Father just like the prodigal son did.

Your witness for Jesus Christ is so simple and uncomplicated. Just put Him first and give Him your best. Let your light shine and see how the darkness is pushed back all around you.

Refresh Today's Priorities

His mercies are new every morning!

Think back over your life and recall the Christians you have known who have just let their light shine by putting God first and giving Him their best. We can all learn something valuable and life-changing from those who have made an impact on our lives—even a small impact. Thank God for these Believers and allow God to use you in the same way today.

The Blessing of Children

Samuel ministered before the Lord, being a child, girded with a linen ephod.

1 Samuel 2:18

Even a little child can be used greatly by the Lord when they learn early to love Him and minister to Him. I am thrilled to see the youth and children in our church on fire for the Lord. It not only blesses me, but seeing them put Him first at such an early age puts me under conviction! I learned this kind of devotion to the Lord later in life, so it is wonderful that they are learning it as children and teens. When godly habits are established early in life, the rest of your life is more productive because you are not hampered by all the distractions and confusion that come from not keeping your focus on the Lord and His will for your life.

Samuel was an extremely effective prophet in Israel, and one of the reasons was because of how he was raised and trained as a very young child. You can read the whole story in 1 Samuel, chapters 1 and 2, of how Samuel was born and raised. God had put the desire in Hannah to have a son, and for years she was barren. She continued to pray and seek the Lord to have a son, and she promised to dedicate him to the Lord. That meant that from the moment he was born, she would teach him that God was to be first place in his life.

It is so important to dedicate our children to God and train them to love and serve Him before anyone or anything else in their lives. By teaching them to put God first, we and they will see the real purpose for their lives. Our children are God's children first. He gives them to us to love, enjoy, train up in His ways—and give back to Him. If we do this, then they will have a deep and lasting understanding of their importance and purpose in life, and we will not be selfish or fleshly in our love for them. Consequently, they will be a great blessing to us and to the Kingdom of God.

Hannah was true to her word. When Samuel was conceived, she probably began to speak to her belly and tell him all about the Lord and how he would go to the temple to serve God as soon as he was weaned. He was a very young boy when she and his father took him to Eli, the priest, to serve the Lord. When the day came for her to part with him, she was not heartbroken. She celebrated the goodness of the Lord in giving her a son. And just so Samuel would not forget how much his parents loved him, every year when they went to worship the Lord at the temple, she took him a new coat. That coat was a constant reminder of how he was dedicated to the Lord before he was even conceived.

The child Samuel ministered unto the Lord before Eli. And the word of the Lord was precious in those days; there was no open vision.

1 Samuel 3:1

Under Eli's instruction Samuel learned how to minister to the Lord and hear from Him. God will put people in your children's lives who will also feed them His Word and teach them about walking in the Spirit. When Samuel was growing up it wasn't like today. We can read the Bible, hear the Word from many different ministers on television, go to church to be fed the Word, and share with one another to get revelation. None of that existed in Samuel's world. The Word was "precious," or scarce, and as a result there was no open vision. No one was seeing in the Spirit or hearing from God.

Samuel did not yet know the Lord, neither was the word of the Lord yet revealed unto him.

1 Samuel 3:7

Even though Samuel did not yet know the Lord or the Word, he ministered to the Lord under Eli's care, and in chapter 3 we have the story of Eli teaching Samuel to recognize the voice of the Lord. One night Samuel was awakened by somebody calling his name. He called back, "Eli, are you calling me?"

Eli said, "No, it's not me." This happened two times, and then a third time. Eli said, "There's something going on with this kid, and I believe it's the Lord." He told Samuel, "If you hear the voice again, say, 'Speak to me, Lord, for I'm Your servant and I hear You.' I believe God is trying to talk to you."

When God spoke to Samuel the fourth time, he answered as Eli had instructed him. God then gave Samuel his first word of prophecy, and from that time on, the Bible says, "And Samuel grew, and the Lord was with him, and did let none of his words fall to the ground" (1 Samuel 3:19). Samuel became one of the most powerful prophets Israel ever had.

Children are important to God, and He will use them in great ways, especially if they are in tune with His Spirit. If He sees them as great gifts, then we need to make it a priority to teach them to put Him first in everything, train them to hear His voice, and feed them His Word. Jesus said it all in Mark 9:42, "Whosoever shall offend one of these little ones that believe in me, it is better for him that a millstone were hanged about his neck, and he were cast into the sea."

Jesus wants all children to come to Him, and it is our responsibility as parents, neighbors and family members to see that they do.

REFRESH TODAY'S PRIORITIES

His mercies are new every morning!

If you have children, maybe you need to evaluate how you are doing and what you are doing to teach them to follow the Holy Spirit and abide in God's Word. They were born to hear His voice and walk in the revelation of His Word—just like you! If you don't have children, pray about getting involved in a child's life. There are so many kids today who don't have godly people in their lives to lead them to Jesus and teach them how to live a prosperous, happy life. You may not know it now, but you might be training up a child who will grow up to be a world evangelist or an amazing teacher of God's Word!

Day 23

YOU ON A SUPERNATURAL DIET

Now the Spirit speaketh expressly, that in the latter times some shall depart from the faith, ….

Forbidding to marry, and commanding to abstain from meats, which God hath created to be received with thanksgiving of them which believe and know the truth.

1 Timothy 4:1, 3

We are in the latter times—a time when imbalance is seen more often than balance—and if there was ever a time to seek God it is now! Who would have thought we would turn on our televisions to see what we see and hear what we hear today. In brilliant color and high definition we can view violence and crime, all kinds of family dysfunctions, sexual and immoral acts—and that's just the news! Paul is telling Timothy that one of the big spiritual issues in the church would be "abstaining from meats, which God hath created to be received with thanksgiving."

Paul said that Christians are to be thankful for and enjoy all the good food God created, but we cannot let food become our first priority. This is hard because not only does it taste good, but also our society revolves around food. Fast-food restaurants are on every corner. There is constant advertising in every kind of media, and every time we celebrate, there are all kinds of tempting foods to see and smell. As a result, a large percentage of Americans are overweight, and many of those Americans are Believers!

We need to learn how to balance food in our lives so that Jesus is always first place. I don't think it's any accident that one of the things God gave us to help us get our priorities straight is fasting. When we fast, we train our minds and hearts to wake up in the morning looking forward to spending time with the Lord instead of looking forward to eating that muffin or biscuit. Fasting is a tool God gave us to make our flesh submit to our spirit and prove that food doesn't dominate us. A fast says to our bodies that Jesus, alone, is Lord.

Fasting can be abused, however, if we do it for "religious" reasons and not to crucify our flesh and draw closer to God. One of the things we do to look more spiritual is fast. Jesus called people who do this hypocrites.

When ye fast, be not, as the hypocrites, of a sad countenance: for they disfigure their faces, that they may appear unto men to fast. Verily I say unto you, They have their reward.

Matthew 6:16

When you fast, do it with a smile on your face! The only reward you will get by starving yourself and dragging yourself around like a martyr to look spiritual is losing a little physical weight. That's not fasting; that's a diet! Without really seeking the Lord and having some joy about it, you won't produce any spiritual growth in your life.

Paul goes on to tell Timothy,

Refuse profane and old wives' fables, and exercise thyself rather unto godliness.

For bodily exercise profiteth little: but godliness is profitable unto all things, having promise of the life that now is, and of that which is to come.

1 Timothy 4:7-8

Now don't use verse 8 as an excuse not to exercise! It does profit you and will keep your temple fit for the Lord's use. What the Holy Spirit is saying is that godliness is the main thing we should pursue. Godliness is the priority because you can't live a godly life apart from God. To be like Him, you have to spend time with Him and get to know Him in His Word. Godly fasting means putting down the desires of our flesh and seeking only the Lord.

I want to live a godly life and not just be saved. My life is more powerful and has more impact if I practice godliness rather than going around telling people I am a Christian. The title means nothing without the fruit, and the fruit doesn't come without abiding in Jesus. (See John 15:1-8.) The purpose of fasting is to bring us closer to Him and put food—or whatever else we might be fasting from—in its proper place and perspective.

Fasting from food comes from a personal conviction from the Holy Spirit that we need to change how we see food and how we use food. It brings godly balance to our eating habits. We cannot make a doctrine out of it and look down our noses at other Believers who aren't fasting or don't fast as much as we do. And we can't get condemned if someone else we know fasts all the time and we don't. Fasting is not like a religious badge to pin on ourselves for being a holier Christian. It is something between God and us. It is a means to purify ourselves and become stronger in Him.

Refresh Today's Priorities

His mercies are new every morning!

What role will food play in your life today? Is it something you think about and talk about all the time? Food is a priority in your life only because it sustains your physical body, which is the temple of the Lord. Ask yourself if food means more to you than it should. God wants you to enjoy it, but He does not want you to plan your life around it or have it dominate your thoughts. If this describes you, pray about fasting. There is nothing like a good fast to put food in its proper place by spending some quality time with the Lord.

Day 24

DIMINISH THE EFFECTS OF A CRITICAL MIND

Whether we live, we live unto the Lord; and whether we die, we die unto the Lord: whether we live therefore, or die, we are the Lord's.

Romans 14:8

We are the Lord's treasured possession, and He wants our lives to be blessed, balanced and fruitful. But He doesn't just snap His fingers and it's done. While He is always faithful and is the author and finisher of our faith (Hebrews 12:2), we have to do our part too. First, we must learn all about Him. He said, "Take my yoke upon you, and learn of me..." (Matthew 11:29). He went on to say in the next verse that this was not a terrible task, that His yoke was easy and His burden was light. He said that when we submitted our lives fully to Him and got to know Him, He would give us rest, and that sounds really good in this stressful world in which we live!

While we are discovering everything we can about Jesus and getting to know Him intimately, we are also discovering who we are in Him. Our eternal destiny is being laid open to us, and we see our purpose and the plan He has for our lives. With that, we must also obey Him and bring our flesh under submission to our spirits. To live a life of balance, a life of temperance that's controlled by the Holy Ghost, we must discipline our bodies. This is the real victory of our lives in Jesus Christ.

Nothing significant is going to happen in our lives if we don't get our flesh under the control of our spirits. Too often we "get in the flesh" and begin to judge one another and criticize one another. A passage of Scripture that reminds us again that we each belong to the Lord, and He has a certain path for each of us, is found in the book of Romans. Although Romans 14 talks a lot about food, the Holy Spirit is really talking about each believer's unique walk with the Lord. Each one of us belongs to Him. If all Believers lived just for Him, He wouldn't have had to write this passage of Scripture! Unfortunately we judge and criticize one another when it is none of our business. I know when I find myself doing this, it means I'm looking at the faults and weaknesses of others so I don't have to deal with my own!

As for the man who is a weak believer, welcome him [into your fellowship], but not to criticize his opinions or pass judgment on his scruples or perplex him with discussions.

One [man's faith permits him to] believe he may eat anything, while a weaker one [limits his] eating to vegetables.

Let not him who eats look down on or despise him who abstains, and let not him who abstains criticize and pass judgment on him who eats; for God has accepted and welcomed him.

Romans 14:1-3 AMP

When Dr. Dollar calls a fast in our church, it can be so easy to look at a sister or brother and say, "Why are you eating that donut? You know the man of God said to fast. You know you're not supposed to eat that donut." We are not supposed to play the role of the Holy Ghost!

Who are you to pass judgment on and censure another's household servant? It is before his own master that he stands or falls. And he shall stand and be upheld, for the Master (the Lord) is mighty to support him and make him stand.

Romans 14:4 AMP

What is the godly priority when it comes to judging and evaluating? What are we supposed to judge first and foremost? Ourselves! When this priority is in place, we will not judge others. I've heard someone say, "Sweep around your own front porch." And Jesus told us to get the beam out of our own eye first. Then we can help get the speck out of another person's eye. (See Luke 6:41-42.) This is a principle of the Kingdom because every Believer answers personally to the Lord. He is their master and they are His servant. We are not their master!

Sometimes we get wrapped up in someone else's problems because we're afraid of facing our own. Romans 14:4 says that the Lord will support us and make us stand tall and strong. He will sustain us as we deal with the issues and face the challenges of our lives. His grace is sufficient for every situation. There's grace to abide in and obey the Word. There's grace to walk in the Spirit. And there's grace to do what the Lord leads us to do by not judging the faults of others and dealing with our own.

Each of us belongs to the Lord, and His path for you is different from His path for me. I cannot judge my life by yours and you cannot judge your life by mine. We must each judge our lives by the Word and how the Spirit is leading us. If we all kept this priority in our lives, we could probably wipe out all strife in the Body of Christ! So continue to walk with Jesus, knowing He is not only your Master, He is every believer's Master. You are the Lord's—and so are they!

REFRESH TODAY'S PRIORITIES

His mercies are new every morning!

Decide that today you will not judge anyone but yourself and see what happens. Allow the Holy Spirit to deal with your attitudes, words and behavior. At the same time, notice if you judge your life by another Believer's life. It's okay to follow them *as* they follow Christ, but you don't want to follow them *instead* of Christ. Today, remember that we all are the Lord's!

Day 25

YOUR BODY IS HIS TEMPLE

I keep under my body, and bring it into subjection: lest that by any means, when I have preached to others, I myself should be a castaway.

1 Corinthians 9:27

In *The Amplified Bible*, this verse reads, "But [like a boxer] I buffet my body [handle it roughly, discipline it by hardships] and subdue it, for fear that after proclaiming to others the Gospel and things pertaining to it, I myself should become unfit [not stand the test, be unapproved and rejected as a counterfeit]." Paul says that he disciplines his body with a godly fear that he should meet the Bible standard of spirituality he has preached to others.

What does this say about fasting? When we honestly seek God through fasting and prayer, we push the flesh aside, deny our appetite's control, and allow our spirit man to develop and to be strengthened. The priority of fasting is to recapture our hunger and rekindle our fire for God. It says to Him, "I am willing to give up anything in order to be in Your presence and to do Your will."

Colossians 1:17 says that Jesus is before all things, and when we fast we enforce that in our lives. Whatever we fast from, whether it is food, our morning latté, or watching football, we are making the statement that He is before it. He is before French fries and surfing the Internet. He is also before the protein shake, green vegetables and baked fish. He's before your diet and wants to direct your diet. He wants your life!

Sometimes our fast turns out to be a total change in lifestyle and eating habits. Food is not supposed to control our lives, and the Lord can reveal cravings that rule our diets. He can show us how He designed our bodies to operate as His temple. First Corinthians 3:16 tells us the importance of this, "Know ye not that ye are the temple of God, and that the Spirit of God dwelleth in you?" The Holy Spirit lives in us to tell us what to eat so we can honor Him with our bodies.

God created our bodies perfectly, every organ working perfectly, but sin caused them to malfunction. We need His wisdom on how to get our bodies healthy and keep them healthy. Yes, there is divine healing; however, there is also divine health. We can walk in divine health if we believe His promise for it and act wisely. James 2:20-26 says that faith without works is dead. If we believe our bodies are healed and in health, then we should eat, drink and exercise accordingly. We should treat the temple of the Lord with respect, because it is the vessel God uses to touch the people in our lives and reveal Himself to them.

For a long time, I watched Creflo take all these vitamins, jumping up in the morning, praising God as he drank his nutrition drink, and it just got on my nerves! We would go out of town and he had this backpack of supplements, and at home he had messed up my beautifully decorated kitchen with all his bottles on the counter. I began to see the importance of what he was doing when God began to show me that my body was His temple, and I needed to take care of it so I could effectively do His will.

I wish I had learned this before I got pregnant! I just ate everything that wasn't nailed down. No temperance. No wisdom on how to care for God's temple. Then, after having the baby, I was fifty or sixty pounds overweight and all out of shape. I had to work so hard to get back to a normal weight and feel good again. Fasting helped me understand the importance of a healthy body. It gave me a godly reverence for it because the Lord lives in my body. I'm His home, and I want Him to be able to move freely in me and through me.

As a minister, I do not want to hinder the work of the Lord by a body that's out of shape, and I don't want to die early and not fulfill my days because I let my flesh have its way! I want to be a vessel of honor for the Lord's use and a great example to those I teach. So I keep my body under submission to the Word and the Spirit and have a godly respect for the body God gave me.

REFRESH TODAY'S PRIORITIES

His mercies are new every morning!

Understand today that everyone's body is different. What may work for your sister or brother may not work for you. Ask the Holy Spirit to put you on His perfect diet and exercise plan for you. You may need to fast to help implement His plan, putting down the flesh and allowing your spirit to dominate. And always remember the priority of fasting: to seek the Lord and His will for your life, to bring new life to your relationship with Him.

Day 26

KEEP TIME ON YOUR SIDE

See then that ye walk circumspectly, not as fools, but as wise, redeeming the time, because the days are evil.

Ephesians 5:15-16

God does not want our lives to be always hit or miss and everything done as a whim of the moment. This is not His idea of a balanced life! He tells us to look carefully how we walk, to take the time to consider where we are, what we are doing, and where we want to go from here. He is instructing us to set goals and make plans to meet those goals. We are not just to wander through life without thinking about what He put us here to accomplish for His Kingdom.

Our lives are not accidents! Some of us may have arrived here because of an accident, but God knew we were coming and already had a great plan for our lives. We are to be diligent and walk with purpose, knowing the meaning of our lives in Him. When we do this, we literally redeem the time in which we are living. The Bible says that we redeem time because the days are evil. In other words, Satan is trying to steal and destroy our time; however, when we walk circumspectly, we take the time God has given us and use it for His purposes. We redeem the time because the enemy can have nothing to do with it!

It is a lie from the enemy that there is nothing spiritual about planning ahead and setting goals. He is just trying to keep you from redeeming the time God has given you to fulfill His plan for your life. You are probably thinking, *But the Bible says in Proverbs 16:9 that we make our plans but God orders our steps. Doesn't that mean that we shouldn't plan anything out? Shouldn't we just live every moment as the Holy Spirit leads us?*

If God is our first priority, we will set our goals and make our plans as He directs us. In Proverbs 16:9 He is not telling us we shouldn't set priorities and make plans. He is just reminding us that we should do it under the direction of the Holy Spirit, and as we walk in the Spirit our plans are subject to His changes. This verse encourages us to stay in constant communication with Him instead of getting a plan, running out the door with it and forgetting about the Lord.

The Bible says that if we walk circumspectly, not only will we redeem our time from the enemy, we will also not be fools! We will be sensible, intelligent people, who know that when we are doing God's will, we are in the place of joy, satisfaction and success. We use every breath we breathe, cognizant of fulfilling the will of God for our lives.

Wherefore be ye not unwise, but understanding what the will of the Lord is.

Ephesians 5:17

When we understand what the will of the Lord is, every day becomes precious. Each moment reveals to us another piece of the puzzle of our lives, as well as how that piece fits into the big picture. We walk circumspectly, looking for opportunities with our families, on our job, when we're at play, or when we see people in the grocery store or the mall to make the most of our time and carry out His will. We continually see ourselves and our lives in the context of the Word of God as the Holy Spirit leads us. We are not thoughtless and vague in our understanding because we have a firm grasp of how God wants us to behave and what He wants us to do.

Jesus talked about walking circumspectly when He gave us the parable of the talents in Luke 19:12-27. God has given each of us gifts and talents to use to further His Kingdom, and we are not to squander them! We are to multiply them for His glory. We are not to bury them and never use them. He calls that evil! Everything He has given us—including time—is to be used to reveal His goodness and love to those around us. We should spend and invest every talent wisely, according to His instructions in His Word and by His Spirit.

When we get right down to the bottom line, our entire contribution to the advancement of the Kingdom of God hinges on how we use the hours allotted to us in the day, in the month, in the years. Our impact for the Kingdom hinges on how we use our time. And we will not use our time wisely and redeem the time for God if we do not walk circumspectly.

Refresh Today's Priorities

His mercies are new every morning!

Today you can have a new perspective on your time by always being aware that only you can redeem your time for God's purpose. Walk circumspectly by asking Him for help in setting goals and forming plans to reach those goals. Are you using the gifts and talents God has given you? Are you making the most of every opportunity to share Jesus with people? And most important, are you always open to the Holy Spirit for a course correction at any moment? I believe that when you walk circumspectly you will not only have a much more productive life, you will also have a happier, more fulfilling time living it.

Day 27

A Spiritually Healthy Heart

"The seed that fell in the weeds—well, these are the ones who hear, but then the seed is crowded out and nothing comes of it as they go about their lives worrying about tomorrow, making money, and having fun.

"But the seed in the good earth—these are the good-hearts who seize the Word and hold on no matter what, sticking with it until there's a harvest."

Luke 8:14-15 THE MESSAGE

If you read through your Bible every year, or if you have ever read through the whole Bible, there is one theme that stands out from Genesis to Revelation: God wants your whole heart. He wants your whole heart because He knows that if your heart is His, then your whole life is His. He's not demanding this because He's a domineering tyrant. He's asking for your whole heart for two reasons. First, because the only way to be saved is by giving Him your whole heart; and second, because giving Him your whole heart every day is the only way you will live a happy and prosperous life—a balanced life.

In Luke, chapter 8, Jesus related the parable of the sower, and then He told His disciples the meaning behind it. He addressed the issue of our hearts. In *The Message* translation, which I have used above, Jesus told us that the "good hearts" are those who grab hold of His Word and never let go until it produces what God has sent it to produce. A good heart, therefore, is essential to receiving everything we need from God and everything He desires to give us.

The Word of God makes it clear that maintaining a good heart is a priority in the Kingdom of God, and if we are going to have a good heart we need to find out from the Word of God how to do that. In verse 14 of Luke 8 in *The Message*, it says that our hearts can be consumed with "worrying about tomorrow, making money and having fun" until these things literally push the Word of God out of our hearts. Therefore, it is important for us to keep our hearts free from these things. Then the soil of our hearts will be of the highest quality and the Word of God will grow in us and transform our lives.

Any gardener or farmer knows that the quality of the soil will determine the growth and quality of the plant. And we must remember that everything in nature reflects the wisdom and character of God himself. In Romans 1:20 it says that the invisible things of God are clearly seen in His creation, even His eternal power and Godhead. We can receive revelation about God's Word from looking at how things grow.

Seeds need good soil to grow into strong, healthy plants and bring forth a great harvest. In the same way the Word of God (the seed) will flourish in a good heart (the soil). In the parable of the sower, Jesus said that God sows the Word in our hearts, and the condition of our hearts determines whether the seed will sprout and grow and thrive. He also told us to watch out for the weeds that would keep our hearts from being good soil: worry, money, and worldly or carnal pleasure.

If we want to keep good hearts, we must get rid of worry the moment we recognize it. We must trust God with whatever it is that is troubling us and continue to walk in faith and confidence, knowing our lives are securely in His hands.

We also need to keep money from capturing our hearts. Jesus warned us in Matthew 6:24 that we could not serve both God and money. When we are believing God for material things or money, we must guard our hearts from coveting the gifts more than the Giver! I believe God wants us to prosper, but we prosper as our soul prospers. (See 3 John 2.) Our soul can prosper only when Jesus is our first love, our first priority and consideration in all matters of life.

Jesus also warned us that worldly or carnal pleasures can choke the Word right out of our hearts. For some of us, especially here in America, this is a big problem! Everywhere we turn we are bombarded with advertising to please ourselves and put our selfish desires above everything else, especially

God. The world encourages us to do everything from eating food we know we shouldn't eat to having sex with everyone we find attractive, to manipulating and lying in order to get what we want. The world tells us, "If it feels good, do it!"

The God who loves us and wants the best for us, however, tells us the truth. Sin is pleasant for a season only! That's how the devil traps us. He gives us great pleasure for a while, then he pulls the rug out from underneath our feet and we fall into a pit of misery. Eventually, sin brings destruction and death. (See Hebrews 11:25 and Romans 6:23.)

Isn't it wonderful that we have a heavenly Father who loves us enough to tell us the truth about these things? He not only warns us that we have an enemy, He also tells us how that enemy will try to attack, trap and destroy us. He puts the Holy Spirit in us to warn us and give us wisdom to overcome every worry, every temptation to love and trust money more than God, and every carnal desire to sin or engage in a destructive behavior. He gave us His Word and His grace to maintain a good heart.

A good heart gladly receives and believes God's Word and rejects any idea or thought that opposes His Word. When we keep good hearts, the Word of God grows into a great harvest in our lives and we are able to be all God wants us to be and do all He has called us to do. We will enjoy the beauty of living a balanced life!

REFRESH TODAY'S PRIORITIES

His mercies are new every morning!

Today is the day to pull the weeds! Are you worried about anything? Is there a financial matter—good or bad—that has totally captured your mind and heart? You know, sometimes it isn't financial problems that crowd out God's Word. Sometimes it is financial success that overshadows the Word and turns our hearts toward money instead of God. What about your flesh? Is it under submission to your spirit and the Holy Spirit, or is there some issue in your life that has put your flesh in control? Examine your heart and see whether or not you are in the faith. (See 2 Corinthians 13:5.) Pull out any weed that would keep your heart from being a heart that pleases God. Then you will have a good heart that will bear much fruit.

Day 28

Life Organization

Unto the angel of the church of Ephesus write; These things saith he that holdeth the seven stars in his right hand, who walketh in the midst of the seven golden candlesticks;

I know thy works, and thy labour, and thy patience, and how thou canst not bear them which are evil: and thou hast tried them which say they are apostles, and are not, and hast found them liars:

And hast borne, and hast patience, and for my name's sake hast laboured, and hast not fainted.

Nevertheless I have somewhat against thee, because thou hast left thy first love.

Revelation 2:1-4

In this passage of Scripture, we find out that Jesus is always walking in our midst. He knows what we are doing and what keeps us so busy that our lives are out of balance. Many of us wear a Christian medal of honor that says, "I'm so busy for the Lord." He must stand there with His arms folded, shaking His head, as we run ourselves ragged doing "His work." We Christian women are baking for the bake sales and potluck suppers. We are working at the thrift shop and food bank to clothe and feed those who are less fortunate than we are. We are running kids to vacation Bible school and all the lessons and activities that will help them develop the gifts God has given them. We are looking for any opportunity to invite someone to church or pray for them. As professionals in the marketplace, we are always striving to be the best at what we do to give honor to our Lord.

Men in the church can be just as busy. They give all they can to their work as a statement of the excellence Jesus brings to their lives. They come home to be super-husbands and super-dads so their families can be super. They go to choir rehearsal and sing in the church choir on Sundays and Wednesdays. They go to the men's meetings. They drive elderly and handicapped people to their doctors' appointments. They coach kids' ball teams and are big brothers and spiritual dads to young people or new Believers.

Running, running and running some more. We get so busy for Jesus that we lose sight of Him! He's right in our midst and we aren't seeing Him or hearing Him. Then we wonder why things go wrong. We scratch our heads, saying, "What are You doing, Lord? Why am I in this mess? I've been doing everything You called me to do."

At that point—usually in a crisis—He's got our full attention! He says, "You've lost your first love." He's talking about Himself. Somewhere in all our grand plans and activities to glorify Him, we turned away from Him. He was there all the time; we were too busy to see Him or to hear Him.

What have you allowed to creep into your life that has caused you to leave your first love, to take your attention from the Lord? Is it your schedule that leaves no room for prayer and study of His Word? Does your job take up most of your time and energy? Are you consumed with relationships with other people or with one person? These are all good things, but have you allowed any of them to get out of the place in which God designed them to be? Are you just too busy?

I don't want my job to be before God. God gave me the job so I could have seed to sow into other people's lives and build His Kingdom, to establish His covenant in the Earth. I don't want money and work to dictate my life; I want Jesus to rule in my heart and mind.

I'm not going to put my family before the Lord either. God gave me my family to love, support, and dedicate to Him. My family is not to get me off course or to be an excuse for not following Him. And there are probably some dead things I need to leave behind if I am really going to follow Him and know Him.

He said unto another, Follow me. But he said, Lord, suffer me first to go and bury my father.

Jesus said unto him, Let the dead bury their dead: but go thou and preach the kingdom of God.

And another also said, Lord, I will follow thee; but let me first go bid them farewell, which are at home at my house.

And Jesus said unto him, No man, having put his hand to the plough, and looking back, is fit for the kingdom of God.

Luke 9:59-62

Jesus wasn't being insensitive or cruel. He was simply pointing out that following Him means that He is always number one in our lives. He is our life. Our thoughts should always be of Him. Our behavior should reflect His character. This happens only through intimacy with Him, and intimacy comes only by spending time with someone.

Then there is money. How busy are you just making money? Remember the rich young ruler? He proudly declared that he had lived a nearly perfect life and was ready to follow Jesus when Jesus said,

If thou wilt be perfect, go and sell that thou hast, and give to the poor, and thou shalt have treasure in heaven: and come and follow me.

But when the young man heard that saying, he went away sorrowful: for he had great possessions.

Then said Jesus unto his disciples, Verily I say unto you, That a rich man shall hardly enter into the kingdom of heaven.

And again I say unto you, It is easier for a camel to go through the eye of a needle, than for a rich man to enter into the kingdom of God.

Matthew 19:21-24

One of the reasons many of us get too busy to know God is because we are afraid we will not have enough money. We can be extremely wealthy and still be afraid of not having enough. Making money has got us by the neck, and fear drives us on. You may say, "Money's not a priority in my life," yet going after it consumes all your time and energy!

You might be one of those who have no time for God or your family because you're doing what God called you to do. You might even be a pastor or a traveling evangelist! One day you wake up and your kids are alienated from you, your spouse is just worn out, and you are lonely and frustrated. Your life is completely out of balance. What happened?

You left your first love through Christian busyness.

There's nothing wrong with being diligent about the Lord's business; we just need to be careful that we don't get too busy. There's a simple test for this. If you're too busy to spend time with Him and your family, then you're too busy.

REFRESH TODAY'S PRIORITIES

His mercies are new every morning!

Today, make a list of all your activities. Then ask the Holy Spirit to confirm that you are right in participating in them. If He confirms that an activity is God's will for you at this time, then don't stop there. Ask Him how much time He wants you to spend on it. Sometimes we give an area of our lives too much time, which distracts us and tires us out so that we don't have that alone, intimate time with the Lord. It is always a good idea to stop from time to time and get a Holy Ghost evaluation! Then you can avoid getting too busy to notice Jesus in your midst.

Day 29

CLEAR COMMUNICATION

He that hath an ear, let him hear what the Spirit saith.

Revelation 2:7

We were created to hear physically, and what an incredible blessing it is to wake up in the morning and hear the birds singing. Our lives are filled with the wonderful sounds of children laughing and music so sweet that it causes our hearts to swell with love for the One who created us. Our hearing also functions as a means to be warned of danger or to learn all kinds of necessary and interesting information. We know that hearing is an essential part of our lives, and those who are deaf have to overcome many difficulties.

When we are born again, our spiritual ears are opened, and we have to learn to hear spiritually. God is a spirit being, we are spirit beings, and we communicate spiritually. We were created by Him to hear His voice in our spirits, to walk with Him and talk with Him every day spirit-to-spirit.

Hearing from God by His Spirit or His Word is the foundation for living a balanced Christian life. As Christians we should never be content with not hearing from God. If we ignore Him when He speaks to us or if we just don't bother to listen for His voice at all, it grieves Him. He is a Father who desires intimacy with His children. He wants to communicate with us, for us to know Him and for Him to know us.

As a mother, if I had children who couldn't hear my voice, that would bother me because they are flesh of my flesh. There is a bond and a desire for relationship that can be achieved only by fellowship and communication with one another, me hearing them and them hearing me. Believe me, I would find other ways of communicating with them like sign language, reading lips, and using the sense of touch if they were unable to hear me.

It would be an even greater grief to me if my children were able to hear my voice but refused to take the time to listen to me. It would be a nightmare to talk to children who continually turned away and gave their attention to someone or something else, especially if I was trying to warn them of impending danger or tell them how to handle a situation they were about to encounter. When we treat the Holy Spirit this way, He is grieved also.

One of the best ways to learn how to hear spiritually is to pray and fast. Prayer and fasting are not so God can hear from us. We can pour our hearts out to Him, but then we must listen because the purpose is so we can hear from Him. Fasting gets our flesh out of the way so we can hear what the Spirit is saying. Fasting is not a spiritual *Let's Make A Deal*—I'll fast and give up all this food and stuff, then God will do what I want Him to do. Fasting doesn't get God's attention because we already have His attention. He lives in us and we live in Him! It doesn't make Him move on our behalf because He's already given us all things that pertain to living a godly life in Christ Jesus. (See 2 Peter 1:3.) Fasting is to move us into a position to hear *Him*.

Hearing from God becomes a lot easier when you realize that God has already made up His mind about you. He rejoices over you and you are His delight. He wants to talk to you. You don't have to beg and plead. You don't have to prove yourself worthy of His attention. He already made it clear that you were worthy by sending His Son to die so that He could adopt you as His own and be with you for eternity. He's thrilled and excited just to see your face and hear your voice, and it is His greatest joy when you make it a priority to take time to commune with only Him.

It takes time for us to grasp and believe how God sees us and feels about us, that He wants to talk with us whether things are going well or we have just made a big mess. We have to understand that we are not holy because of what we say or do. We are holy because of the blood of Jesus. That's how God sees us, and we need to see ourselves that way. Then we won't think it strange that our Father would talk to us because we are His kids!

If you saw me with my kids and observed that I never spoke to them, you would probably assume I wasn't their mother. But I am their mother and I talk with them all the time. That's the way your Father wants to talk with you!

Refresh Today's Priorities

His mercies are new every morning!

When was the last time you had a heart-to-heart talk with your Father? Have you ever felt unworthy to talk with Him? Today, take some time to allow the Holy Spirit to show you that He wants to speak to you no matter what condition you *think* you are in or really *are* in. Open your heart and mind to receive whatever He wants to give you: revelation, wisdom, instruction, a correction, or a shot of encouragement. Sometimes all we need is a simple revelation that He wants to talk to us which prompts us to open our hearts and be healed and restored. Those are the moments that change our lives!

Day 30

REJUVENATE YOUR THOUGHTS

Therefore take no thought, saying, What shall we eat? or, What shall we drink? or, Wherewithal shall we be clothed?

(For after all these things do the Gentiles seek:) for your heavenly Father knoweth that ye have need of all these things.

But seek ye first the kingdom of God, and his righteousness; and all these things shall be added unto you.

Matthew 6:31-33

Every unbeliever is consumed with what they will eat, drink and wear. The world runs on acquiring the things people need to survive and that they believe will give them pleasure. That is why the world is out of balance. It takes no thought of God, who is perfect balance and harmony, and takes only thought for itself.

In these verses Jesus is telling us not to have the mindset of the natural man, who thinks only about himself and his needs and desires. Jesus says God already knows what we need, so we shouldn't take that thought. We cannot let that be our mindset. Instead, we should seek first, aim at, and strive after His

Kingdom and His righteousness (His way of doing and being right) and then all these things we need and desire will come to us.

Jesus then says, "Take therefore no thought for the morrow: for the morrow shall take thought for the things of itself" (Matthew 6:34). This is one of the keys to thinking like God, speaking like God, and acting like God. Don't worry about tomorrow! For example, you can consider your options prayerfully and get the direction of the Holy Spirit on paying your bills, but don't worry and wring your hands about how the bills are going to get paid. Seek God first, and God will take care of you.

We have to trust our Father. We've got to get rid of that mindset that says, "I've got to take care of myself because that's what I've always done and no one else is going to do it if I don't." No, that mindset died when we were born again and became children of the Most High God. We are no longer our own little gods because we belong to Him. And when our lives are fully yielded to His will and we seek Him before all else—not worrying—then everything we need in life will be added to us.

To be God-conscious or God-inside-minded takes some effort. Nothing just changes by itself, and our minds are no different. To live as a God-conscious person instead of a self-conscious person requires some study and meditation on our part, and then His Word and the Holy Spirit transform us and balance us. This is how we learn to think like He thinks and do things the way He does them. Jesus was our perfect example. He demonstrated how a human being who is born again and has a mind renewed by God's Word conducts themselves by studying the Scriptures, praying, obeying and sticking close to the Father.

If we are living in discouragement and defeat, it is our fault. It's not the government, our boss, or our rebellious child that is making us miserable. We are allowing ourselves to be miserable by not taking all those miserable thoughts captive! We believe everything but the Word of God about ourselves and our situation. Consequently, we perceive our situation from every vantage point but God's. And God's perspective is the only one that will bring peace and the answers we need to move forward in our lives.

To live in joy and victory we must change our minds. When we change our minds, we will make better decisions and our lives will improve. Quit blaming the devil! Quit blaming your spouse. Quit blaming everybody else and take responsibility for your own stinkin' thinkin'. If you want to function like Jesus, you are going to have to think like Jesus. And that happens only when you immerse your eyes and ears and mind and heart in God's Word. Doing this makes you conscious of God all the time, and being God-conscious adds all His blessings because you are continually seeking His Kingdom and His righteousness.

We are not meant to always struggle, barely getting by, living from paycheck to paycheck, sick and afraid of dying, about to lose our minds with worry, our kids driving us crazy, and our jobs draining us of every ounce of strength. That's the way the world lives, and that's the way Christians live when they do not renew their minds with God's Word and become God-conscious.

I see two extremes in the Body of Christ: those who believe God should do everything and those who believe they should do everything. The balance and truth are in the middle, and we get to the middle by being God-conscious, by knowing that He's our Father and we are His children, and we are in this together. We do our part and He does His. It's a relationship that we develop by renewing our minds with God's Word and learning to think like He thinks.

When we were born again and became new creatures, old things passed away and everything became new—in our spirits. (See 2 Corinthians 5:17.) Now our souls have to catch the revelation of that and begin to live in it. The Word of God and the Spirit of God bring that revelation from our heads (as we renew our minds) to our hearts (where we believe) and then we are transformed. We are God-conscious.

Believers who renew their minds live like Jesus, not worrying about tomorrow, just following the Spirit and abiding in the Word of God. Being God-conscious, they live the abundant, balanced life Jesus died to give them—and so can you!

REFRESH TODAY'S PRIORITIES

His mercies are new every morning!

Have you set a time each day when you not only read your Bible, you study it? If not, do it! Look up the meanings of the Greek and Hebrew words in a concordance. Read commentaries on the passages you study. Then meditate on the things you learned until you come back to it the next day. Let the Holy Spirit teach you, and you will become more and more God-conscious.

Day 31

BOOST YOUR LEVEL OF JOY

The kingdom of God is not meat and drink; but righteousness, and peace, and joy in the Holy Ghost.

Romans 14:17

Did you know that joy was a priority in the Kingdom of God? This verse declares that the Kingdom of God *is* joy! Jesus said that we are to seek first the Kingdom of God (Matthew 6:33), so that means joy is a top priority in living our Christian lives. When we are filled with His joy, we are strong, stable and balanced. People around us will know we are followers of Jesus because we have joy.

In both the Old and New Testaments, joy is a main theme with God. In fact, one of the characteristics of God is joy. Zephaniah 3:17 says, "The Lord thy God in the midst of thee is mighty; he will save, he will rejoice over thee with *joy;* he will rest in his love, he will *joy* over thee with singing." God sings and rejoices over us with joy! King David, who had a heart after God's heart, instructed his singers and musicians to lift up their voices with joy. (See 1 Chronicles 15:16.) As New

Covenant Believers, a fruit of the Spirit is joy. We are to be like our Father God and always walk in joy.

Keeping the joy of the Lord makes it easy to maintain a good attitude. After all, what good has it ever done to walk around feeling and looking like you were a total wreck? You may have gotten a little sympathy from people, but losing your joy in God never solves anything and can even set you back because the joy of the Lord is your strength (Nehemiah 8:10). Without strength, you can't accomplish much of anything for the Kingdom of God.

When you have some joy about you, you look good and are a blessing to the people you meet. How many people love to see a sad, troubled face coming toward them? Not many! When I see a person who is obviously worn out and beat down with cares, I have compassion for them, and my first objective in ministering to them is to help them get back the joy of the Lord. If they get their joy back, they will have God's strength and wisdom to deal with their problems.

What does it take to keep your joy in the Lord? The answer is found in Romans 14:17: "joy in the Holy Ghost." Joy is one of the fruits of the Spirit, so we develop joy in our lives by spending time praying in the Spirit, listening to the Spirit and communing with the Spirit in God's Word. The more contact we have with the Holy Spirit, the more joy we will have in our lives. And the more joy we have in our lives, the more joy we can bring to the people around us.

We also need to walk out our everyday lives with the Holy Ghost. We don't leave Him in our prayer closet and go about our business alone. No! He lives in us and goes with us wherever we go. If we don't talk with Him and consult with Him throughout our day, we are not taking advantage of the greatest blessing in our lives. He is our Teacher, Comforter and Guide through life. He possesses all wisdom and knowledge, all power and love. It is just plain stupid not to tap into all that!

My family and friends can tell when I'm walking in the Spirit—and they also can tell when I'm not! If I have gone off into my own thinking and am operating independently of the Spirit, chances are I have taken the weight of the world on my shoulders, the smile is off my face and joy is nowhere to be found. I'm dragging around because I have no strength. This is not a pretty sight!

God never created human beings to live in sorrow, despair and weakness. He created us to be joyful, to enjoy the life He has given us. His Word says, "Rejoice in the Lord alway: and again I say, Rejoice" (Philippians 4:4). Always means always! We are literally commanded to be filled with the joy of the Lord at all times. Psalm 16:11 says, "Thou wilt shew me the path of life: in thy presence is fulness of joy; at thy right hand there are pleasures for evermore." If you want the fullness of joy, stay in His presence!

Walk in the Spirit! Then you will have not only strength but revelation. In His presence, where there is fullness of joy, is where He shows you the path and plan for your life. This is where you find out who you really are and what you are called to do. Best of all, this is also where "there are pleasures evermore." God's pleasures last!

When you begin to live according to godly priorities, one of the things you come to realize is that every priority in the Christian life points to the number one priority: putting Jesus first in everything and at all times. Joy is no exception. You cannot maintain joy unless you are walking in the Spirit, and you cannot walk in the Spirit unless Jesus Christ is your first priority.

REFRESH TODAY'S PRIORITIES

His mercies are new every morning!

Today, why don't you try to check your level of joy at least once every hour? God doesn't expect you to be *emotionally happy* at all times, but He gave you the ability to be *spiritually joyful* no matter what is going on in your life. You will have hard times and heartache in life because we all do, yet at the same time—deep in your heart where the Holy Spirit abides—

you always have His joy, which is His strength. His joy is what keeps you going in both good times and bad times. No matter what you face today, draw upon the joy of the Lord and be strong in Him.

Day 32

Nourishment for Your Spirit

Then said he unto him, A certain man made a great supper, and bade many:

And sent his servant at supper time to say to them that were bidden, Come; for all things are now ready.

And they all with one consent began to make excuse.

Luke 14:16-18

God is continuously bidding you to come and dine with Him. Did you know that? He always has a table prepared for you, and it is covered with the most nutritious, soul-strengthening food you could ever imagine. That food, of course, is His holy Word. He has tremendous revelation just waiting for you! All you have to do is sit down at His table and eat with Him.

Unfortunately, just like the people in the parable Jesus told in Luke, chapter 14, most of us have all these excuses why we can't sit down with the Holy Spirit and spend some time in His Word. Our excuses are the same ones Jesus named, so let's take a look at them.

They all with one consent began to make excuse. The first said unto him, I have bought a piece of ground, and I must needs go and see it: I pray thee have me excused.

Luke 14:18

Jesus said this man's possessions and financial investments were more important than coming to dine with Him. What possessions have you allowed to take you away from the Word of God? That house you believed God for, that you prayed for? Do you spend all your time admiring it and enjoying it instead of going to church to feast on the Word or taking time to study the Word? Do you spend more time washing and cleaning your car than you spend with the Lord? Are you at the computer for hours, checking the stock market and what's for sale on various Web sites?

Possessions, things that are important to us, have the potential to take us away from the Word of God. Before long, we notice that our minds are clouded and our emotions are in turmoil. All this happens because our spirits are malnourished. We have not sat at the Lord's table to partake of the spiritual food He has for us.

Many of us say, "Well, I spend a lot more time in church and reading my Bible than the rest of my family and friends." But we can't judge our lives by comparing them with everyone else. This is a matter strictly between us and God. If He is truly our first priority, then we will let Him tell us how much time we should spend in the Word each day and how much time we should spend taking care of the possessions He has given us. As long as we remember that we are simply stewards over His possessions, that everything we have is His as well as ours, then we won't miss the feast He has for us!

Another said, I have bought five yoke of oxen, and I go to prove them: I pray thee have me excused.

Luke 14:19

This man had a great excuse! He said that he had work to do. He had to make a living and support his wife and family. He had to fulfill the call of God on his life. How many of us have justified neglecting the Word of God and not applying the Word to our daily lives because we were busy doing what He called us to do? Whether we are a manager at a convenience store or a doctor or a pulpit minister, it is so easy to keep moving and not stop to eat from the Lord's table. As a result, we find ourselves spiritually bankrupt one day because we cannot live by physical bread alone.

It is important to fulfill God's call on our lives; however, we cannot do that effectively or gain any real satisfaction and joy in doing it if we do not take the time to allow the Holy Spirit to reveal His Word to us. No matter what we are called to do at any given season of our lives, the success of doing that always depends on receiving steady revelation from the Word of God and instruction from the Holy Spirit. There are no shortcuts in the Kingdom of God!

Another said, I have married a wife, and therefore I cannot come.

Luke 14:20

This is probably the most compelling of all the excuses because this man was actually referring to the Old Testament law, which said, "When a man hath taken a new wife, he shall not go out to war, neither shall he be charged with any business: but he shall be free at home one year, and shall cheer up his wife which he hath taken" (Deuteronomy 24:5). How many of us have used the Word of God to avoid studying the Word of God? The fact that Jesus used this in His parable shows that He knows just how clever we can be to try to get out of spending time studying His Word!

Certainly a spouse is a priority, but we can't put our mates before the Word of God. After having faith for the mate God brought to us, we cannot drop Him and put all our time and energy toward our spouse. We should never make our husband or wife the center of our world instead of God. Any Believer who is married knows that marital bliss is not going to last long unless Jesus Christ is at the center of the marriage. Eventually, the reality of living with another flawed human being will set in! It isn't long before we realize our lives are still not perfect, and

the only way our marriage—or any relationship in our lives—
will work is to turn it over to God and partake of His Word.

In 1 Corinthians 7:29 Paul says, "But this I say, brethren,
the time is short: it remaineth, that both they that have wives
be as though they had none." He is not telling husbands to
ignore their wives! He is speaking in context of living for the
Lord, and what he means is that married people should be just
as devoted to God after they are married as they were before
they were married.

When I first married Creflo, I got so angry and upset with
him because I didn't feel that I was as important to him as I
should be. I didn't understand why he was so intent on
pleasing God and developing the ministry God had given him.
He would travel all around the world while I was pregnant,
and I thought he should be at home with me, holding my hand
and telling me how great I was. He wasn't cold or insensitive to
me, but I saw it that way because I had put him at the center of
my world instead of God. I was looking to Creflo for love,
security and value, instead of looking to God.

It took some time, but eventually I got so miserable that I
had to look to God instead of my husband for my happiness.
When I began to do that, it wasn't long before Creflo looked
better and better to me! It is amazing how your situation can
stay the same, but how you relate to it and the people in it
change drastically simply because you now see it and them

through the eyes of God and His Word instead of your selfish desires and fears.

Without spiritual food, which is the Word of God, we cannot walk in the Spirit and live a victorious, balanced life in this world. Therefore, we must take every opportunity we can to partake of God's Word and receive the revelation we need. It does us no good to make excuses because Jesus knows them all anyway! Instead of wasting effort trying to find an excuse, we should go straight to the Word of God and partake of the meal He has for us at that moment.

REFRESH TODAY'S PRIORITIES

His mercies are new every morning!

Take a good look at your daily schedule of activities. Did some of the things I mentioned above make you uncomfortable? How much time do you spend taking care of your possessions, like your home, yard, car, boat, computer, sports equipment, etc.? Evaluate your working hours. There are times when overtime is necessary, but it should be the exception and not the rule. If you are married, does your spouse captivate your thoughts, and are they the center of your life? Make sure your possessions, your work and your spouse have the correct place in your heart today. Each one of these parts of your life should be viewed through God's eyes!

Day 33

A New and Fresh Attitude

Consequently, from now on we estimate and regard no one from a [purely] human point of view [in terms of natural standards of value]. [No] even though we once did estimate Christ from a human viewpoint and as a man, yet now [we have such knowledge of Him that] we know Him no longer [in terms of the flesh].

Therefore if any person is [ingrafted] in Christ (the Messiah) he is a new creation (a new creature altogether); the old [previous moral and spiritual condition] has passed away. Behold, the fresh and new has come!

2 Corinthians 5:16-17 AMP

These verses describe the most important and radical change a human being can undergo. Receiving Jesus Christ as your Lord and Savior should cause an absolute revolution in the way you think, how you talk to others, and the way you conduct yourself. Getting saved is not just a passport to Heaven; it is a complete transformation of your character and behavior. Your redemption establishes you in a new, balanced life.

As the song says, you have a new attitude!

Unfortunately, when God saved us, He did not save us from our old attitudes. That's what we have to change. When I got married, I thought that going from my parents' house to my husband's house would automatically change my attitude. You know how it is when you go into marriage with these fantasies about how things are going to be perfect. But then I began to hear my husband say some of the same things that my father had said about my attitude! I needed to check it, it needed to be changed, and it needed to line up with God's Word.

The same thing happens when we are born again. We move from the old, dead spiritual house to a new, alive-unto-God spiritual house, but we take our old attitudes with us. Thank God the Holy Spirit lives in that new house with us! He can help us get rid of those attitudes and help us rid ourselves of ungodly thinking and behaving.

Some Believers may have been on drugs or cigarettes, and when they got saved they instantly lost all craving for them. This kind of healing and deliverance is great, but it doesn't mean they don't need to go through the process of changing their attitudes and the way they think. If they don't fill their clean house with the Word of God, they will have no strength or wisdom to keep the enemy from putting them in bondage again. (See Luke 11:24-26.)

Some Believers are not instantly and completely set free, so in order to get free in the first place, they learn the process and disciplines of changing the way they think and adopting Christlike attitudes. But whether we are instantly and completely delivered or we are set free through the process, all Believers have to make the choice to go through the process of adopting a new attitude, a Jesus attitude.

We go through this process to please the Lord and become more like Him, not to look good in front of our brothers and sisters or impress the boss at work. We can't even change our attitude because our pastor tells us to. We have to do it because we know it is the right thing to do, and it is the right thing for us. Third John 2 says that we will prosper to the degree that our souls prosper, and our souls are not prospering if we have an ugly, ungodly attitude!

The old, unregenerate you had an attitude that was selfish and self-centered, negative and fearful. Now, you are new on the inside. Your spirit has a new attitude that is loving, giving, positive, loves to serve others, and is filled with faith in a Father God who can do anything. This is what you want to bring from the inside to the outside, from your inward man to your outward man. You do this by doing what Joshua and Caleb did when they went into the Promised Land to spy it out. (See Numbers 13 and 14.) They looked at the situation and maintained a godly attitude by believing God's Word over anything else they saw or experienced. They saw the giants and the great cities, but God had said that the land was theirs. They chose to believe Him.

When you choose to believe and live according to God's Word instead of your carnal reasoning and circumstances, your attitude will be spiritually right. You will mind the things of the Spirit instead of the flesh. As a result, like Caleb and Joshua, you will enjoy God's life and peace.

> **They that are after the flesh do mind the things of the flesh; but they that are after the Spirit the things of the Spirit.**
>
> **For to be carnally minded is death; but to be spiritually minded is life and peace.**
>
> **Romans 8:5-6**

This is what your new attitude will produce: life and peace! And "life" is not referring to just breathing; it is talking about the abundant life, the God-kind of life that is blessed and productive and a joy to live. This is not just living for the weekends. This is pure life that lasts 24/7 and comes only from knowing God, life that is far superior to and supersedes anything this world can offer.

Do you have the attitude that says, "Jesus is my life, and my life is incredible," or are you just repeating religious jargon like a parrot? Do you believe what God says or don't you? If you believe Him, your attitude will change. You will have a Jesus attitude by believing what God says in His Word, just like

Joshua and Caleb did. And remember, they were the ones who took the Promised Land!

Refresh Today's Priorities

His mercies are new every morning!

Make a list of the things that bother you, and you will probably find the attitudes you need to change! Keep in mind that you will be changed only by lining up your thoughts about these issues with the Word of God. Change what you believe concerning them, and you will change your attitude.

Day 34

IMPROVE THE CONDITION OF YOUR WORK

Prepare thy work without, and make it fit for thyself in the field; and afterwards build thine house.

Proverbs 24:27

Growing up is a constant battle and education in keeping our balance in God. This is a fantastic scripture for young people because it talks about figuring out who they are and what God has called them to do before they get married. When an engaged couple knows what God has called each of them to do, that's half the battle. They have a good idea from the beginning of their marriage what each of them will be pursuing throughout their lifetime. No one wants to be married to someone who completely opposes their calling or has no appreciation for their gifts. Married people should be an encouragement to one another and not a stumbling block.

This verse is also saying that a young man who wants to be able to provide for his wife and eventually for his children should establish himself in a job or career before he gets married. This is something we always encourage because he may marry a career woman, but when those babies start coming she may not want to remain a career woman! He has to be able to bear the responsibility of supporting the family.

A lot of young men look at their jobs and how much money they make as status symbols or their ticket to being respected and admired by other people. Even in the church we see this happen: men running like there's no tomorrow, trying to get ahead while their wife and children never see them. But God doesn't see it that way. He wrote Proverbs 24:27 because after Him, a man's wife and children are his next priority. One of the main reasons God gives gifts and callings to men is so they can take good care of their families.

Then there are some who use the things of God to be irresponsible toward their families. I don't care how sanctified and holy a man carries on, if his wife and children are suffering because his nose is always in the Bible and he's not making a living, he needs to meditate on Proverbs 24:27! In case you think what I have been saying is just Old Covenant, here is a powerful verse of Scripture from the New Testament.

If any provide not for his own, and specially for those of his own house, he hath denied the faith, and is worse than an infidel.

1 Timothy 5:8

Obviously there were men in Paul's time that were not providing for their wives and children. Paul said those who do this have denied their faith in Jesus Christ and are acting worse than unbelievers! If you are guilty of this, then you need to repent and make it a priority to get a job and take good care of your family.

If you are already taking good care of your family, and you had any doubts as to the importance of what you are doing in God's eyes—this is great news! You can take a godly pride in what you are doing and pray with confidence. Yes, I just said that you can pray with confidence because the Bible says that when a husband honors his wife and treats her well, God will hear his prayers.

> **Likewise, ye husbands, dwell with them according to knowledge, giving honour unto the wife, as unto the weaker vessel, and as being heirs together of the grace of life; that your prayers be not hindered.**
>
> **1 Peter 3:7**

How many men are suffering in life, never getting ahead or accomplishing their dreams, simply because they are not putting God first and then their wife and children second? They work and work, ignoring their families, and even if they do achieve financial success, their professional goals or have a successful ministry, in the end that is all they have. That is not the way God desires them to live. He desires to give them abundant life, but He cannot do that if their priorities are not right.

In most cases, priorities are not right because heart motivations are not lined up with God's Word. When you put your relationship with God and His Word first, then your spouse and children, then your job (which can also be your ministry), you will be happy and fulfilled in your life.

Women are not exempt from Proverbs 24:27! How many times do we see a young woman marry the wrong guy simply because she didn't wait long enough to see if he could plow his field and build the house for her to live in? I'm not saying he has to be a millionaire and own a mansion before she marries him, but she should see a long enough track record of responsible behavior before committing to live the rest of her life with him. Believe me, his great looks and charming personality are not going to thrill you when you have a toddler and a baby and he won't get a job!

Young women also need to keep in mind that Proverbs 24:27 does not exempt them from finding out who they are in Christ and what God has called them to do. First Corinthians 12:12-27 talks about how every member of the Body of Christ is important, and God sets each one of us—male and female— in the call He desires us to fulfill. Most women look forward to marriage and having children, and they make their husbands and children a priority in their lives. They also have gifts and talents God gave them, which should not be neglected. God gave them these gifts for His purposes.

When a man and a woman have a clear understanding of who they are and what each of them has been called by God to do, then they can have a marriage that brings joy and success to themselves, their children and everyone around them. There are couples who marry knowing only that God has brought them together, and their gifts and callings emerge as they walk with the Lord, together. But generally, when we are still single, it is wise to prepare our work without, get an understanding from the Lord about our purpose in life, before entering into marriage and having a family.

REFRESH TODAY'S PRIORITIES

His mercies are new every morning!

Have you really plowed your field, yet? If you don't know what God has called you to do, ask Him! Knowing what you are supposed to be doing brings great balance into your life. The Holy Spirit may not tell you everything, but He will give you the next step to take. His desire is for you to be content and to take joy in what you do in life. He wants to bless your family through you. He wants you to walk in the greatness He put in you when you received Jesus as your Lord and Savior. Today, let your eyes and ears be open to receive His direction for your life.

Day 35

LOSING WEIGHTS

Therefore then, since we are surrounded by so great a cloud of witnesses [who have borne testimony to the Truth], let us strip off and throw aside every encumbrance (unnecessary weight) and that sin which so readily (deftly and cleverly) clings to and entangles us, and let us run with patient endurance and steady and active persistence the appointed course of the race that is set before us.

Hebrews 12:1 AMP

It is hard to run a race and win if we have all kinds of weights hanging on us. Talk about imbalance! We can still participate in the race; however, we will not enjoy it very much, and it is unlikely we will win. A weight to the Christian is simply anything that takes us away from God. That's why He told us to lay aside those things. Lay aside the sin that wants to cling to us, entangle us, bind us up, and get us off focus to the point where we are no longer putting God first. Instead, something else has become first and is weighing us down in our race.

We have lots to do as Believers! We are continuously throwing off weights and sins and training our eyes to stay glued to Jesus, who is our leader and source of our faith, and who is bringing us to maturity in Him.

Looking away [from all that will distract] to Jesus, Who is the Leader and the Source of our faith [giving the first incentive for our belief] and is also its Finisher [bringing it to maturity and perfection]. He, for the joy [of obtaining the prize] that was set before Him, endured the cross, despising and ignoring the shame, and is now seated at the right hand of the throne of God.

Hebrews 12:2 AMP

The *King James Version* calls Jesus the "author and finisher of our faith." From these verses of Scripture, it is obvious that God does not want any of His children to live at a disadvantage. He wants us to have everything we need to run our race, and He gives us all His wisdom and strength to run it well. This is the abundant life Jesus died to give us!

When we talk about abundant life, all kinds of things come to mind; but the abundance God gives us also has a purpose, a purpose we can never lose sight of. Each of us has a part to play in the harvest of souls God is drawing in these last days. Each of us has a harvest of souls crying out, "Please, come show me the way! Give me the truth! Reveal the eternal love and life of God to me!"

Our Promised Land is not just a nice house and car, a happy and healthy family, and an enjoyable and successful career. Our Promised Land is the people we will influence for Jesus Christ. I don't mean to beat you over the head; it's important to get things right in our lives because the harvest is on the line. God can't take us into our Promised Land if we continue running around in the wilderness, fussing and fighting with folks, not walking in love or holding to the truth of God's Word. It's time to lay aside those weights that are holding us back and please Jesus instead of ourselves.

Some people in the church want to live a life that doesn't have any impact on people's lives. It doesn't matter to them if their lives never reflect anything about God. My opinion is, they might not be truly saved; at best, they are saved and are settling for so little. There is a higher calling and a richer life that reaches for perfection in Jesus and makes a powerful impact on this world. As for me, I prefer to "press toward the mark for the prize of the high calling of God in Christ Jesus" (Philippians 3:14). I want to win that race and capture that prize.

I don't want to cross the finish line alone. I want to fly across that finish line bringing hundreds of thousands of souls into the Kingdom of God. The only way I can do that is to keep from being bound by and getting entangled with the things of this world. For example, God put me in check about how I related to my business life. He said, "Don't get all sidetracked with it. Remember My purposes in it. Keep it all in context of My will for your life and don't go off and try to create your own significance and financial security. I am the author and finisher of your faith!"

God wants us to prosper in everything we do. He also wants us to keep that prosperity in godly perspective. Otherwise, it will become a weight that will hold us back and keep us from doing our part in this last days' harvest. Make no mistake about it, people are God's priority. He proved that by sending Jesus to die for our sin so that we could be reconciled to Him. That's how much the harvest means to Him!

REFRESH TODAY'S PRIORITIES

His mercies are new every morning!

If Jesus gave His life for the harvest, what do you believe you should give for the harvest? There are Christians all over the world, and throughout the life of the Church, who have given their lives for the harvest. In most cases, however, giving your life has much more to do with the little things. Do you obey the unction of the Holy Ghost when He tells you to talk to a stranger? Do you stop to pray for those who are sick or distressed over something? This is giving your life! This is not being distracted and weighed down by the things of this world, but looking to Jesus at all times. You will never know until you get to Heaven how many lives came into His loving arms simply because you gave your life—one moment at a time.

Day 36

YOUR DAILY RÉGIME IN CHRIST

"I have been crucified with Christ; and it is no longer I who live, but Christ lives in me; and the life which I now live in the flesh I live by faith in the Son of God, who loved me and gave Himself up for me.

Galatians 2:20 NASB

As we have pastored over the years, unfortunately we have observed that too many Believers do not follow Jesus Christ in the manner God wants them to. If He doesn't fit into their box, giving them everything they want and only requiring a certain amount of their time and energy, they lay Him aside. They want to make God into their idea of what He should be instead of finding out who He really is, how He thinks, the way He does things, and what He likes and doesn't like. They want Him to please them instead of pleasing Him.

Our heavenly Father loves us and will try to bless us in every way; however, He will not violate His character and holy nature just to please us. When you think about it a moment, it is the utmost ignorance to believe you can make God into what you want Him to be. Being a child of God is not about Him fitting into our box; it is about our becoming like Him and allowing Him to be the Lord of every area of our lives.

Paul said it best. "It is no longer I who live, but Christ lives in me, and the life which I now live in the flesh I live by faith in the Son of God." I believe that if every Christian truly understood and embraced this truth, the Body of Christ would be what it should be: the powerful, effective, and productive Church that the gates of Hell could not withstand.

Unfortunately, we still have a lot of people in our midst who continue to cling to their selfish interests and agendas, causing strife and division or simply never contributing anything. They are imbalanced because they haven't faced the fact that God is not going to adapt to them; they must adapt their lives to Him and His Word.

God desires you to be who He created you to be. You don't have a clue about that if you are holding on to the person you think you want to be or think you ought to be. It is interesting that in Matthew 16:25 Jesus didn't say, "If you give Me your life, you will get it back." He said, "If you give Me your life, you will *find* it." There is a big difference, and I'm so glad there is! I don't want *my* idea for my life; I want *His* idea for my life. Every day as I get into His Word, pray and commune with the Holy Spirit, I find out more and more about who I am in Him. Now, *that* is exciting!

Periodically you have to look at your life and see if you are really who God wants you to be and are doing what He's called you to do. Once I looked at all the different things I was doing—starting up this new business, doing interior design on the side, trying to manage a record company, traveling, raising kids—and God said, "What are you doing?" He stopped me in my tracks and got me to consider why I was doing all this stuff.

I had to be honest and ask myself, "Am I trying to do all these things to establish my own significance as a woman in the business world? What am I trying to accomplish? Who am I competing with? Am I trying to be better than somebody else? What really is the issue here?" I realized I was just being a good Girl Scout, going after my badge of spirituality and trying to be Christian Superwoman. I was doing what I thought I needed to do to be respected and admired as a woman and as a Believer, but I wasn't *finding my life* in Him.

When I started letting the Holy Spirit direct me and set my schedule and priorities, I began to find out a lot more about Him and about who I really was. I discovered He longs to hear my voice and loves to have fellowship with me. He cherishes every moment we spend together, and He takes great delight in working out my problems with me, giving me wisdom and revelation that I would never have known had I not stopped to listen to Him and then to obey His instructions.

If I had continued doing what I thought I should be doing, I shudder to think where I might be today! I may have become successful by the world's standards and even by some Christians' standards, but I certainly wouldn't be as content, as fulfilled and as intimate with Him as I am now. Moreover, I wouldn't have the confidence that I was truly on the right track in my life. The only way you can have that confidence is to accept the fact that your life is not yours. Your life is His.

This is hard for a lot of us. We want to be a certain way and do certain things, and we are afraid that if we give it all to Him, He will make us into someone we don't want to be or have us doing something we have no passion for or do not value. The enemy loves to sit on our shoulders and tell us how terrible our lives will be if we turn them completely over to God. He'll say, "You will never have any fun again. No one will want to be around you or be able to relate to you because you'll be such a fanatical Jesus freak. You'll be like one of those crazy Christians who say and do horrible things in so many movies you've seen."

The world produces movies and television shows that present Christians as deranged and insane; that is the devil's propaganda. He inspires these things just to turn people away from Jesus, who is gentle, compassionate and loving. He is wise and of perfect character and integrity. Most important, He died for all of our sins. He made a way for us to be reconciled to the Father.

Whenever the devil tries to tell you that you will become a crazy idiot if you turn your whole life over to God, point to the cross and call him the liar that he is! When you give your life fully to God, the truth is, you will become more and more like Jesus; and He is the most sane, complete, perfect human being who ever walked this Earth.

He said to all, If any person wills to come after Me, let him deny himself [disown himself, forget, lose sight of himself and his own interests, refuse and give up himself] and take up his cross daily and follow Me [cleave steadfastly to Me, conform wholly to My example in living and, if need be, in dying also].

Luke 9:23 AMP

People always think that "taking up their cross" means something huge and horrible like being persecuted, tortured and dying for Jesus. Some Christians have had to face these things through the centuries of the Church, but most of us—especially in America—take up our crosses in a whole different way. Jesus said it: "Let him deny himself." Our cross is to deny ourselves and follow Him. We are to follow Him all day long and not just a couple of hours a week while we are in church. We are to give up that meal or that movie or that shopping trip if necessary in order to follow Him. We are to take up whatever He instructs us to take up.

Jesus was the best example of denying yourself. He denied Himself so many things, including a long life, in order to fulfill God's will. He could have just done what He wanted to do. He was a carpenter and probably had a pretty profitable business. We know He was good at it because He created the heavens and the Earth and God said it was all good! However, being a carpenter and building a successful business was not His purpose. Living a long life and having a wife and family were not His destiny. He laid all that aside to do the will of God.

People didn't understand Jesus either. The religious people hated Him and thought He was crazy most of the time. Some said He had demons in Him, and others would hear His messages and just shake their heads because everything He said was too deep for them. He gave up a good reputation and laid His earthly life aside for the will of God. And He did it all for us!

Taking up our cross is a hard thing to do, but what a wonderful opportunity we have of showing Jesus how much we love Him! And He has made this a win-win situation for us. By taking up our cross and following Him, by denying ourselves, we find ourselves! Our lives easily fall into perfect balance. Every day becomes an adventure in discovering who we are and the amazing plan He has for our lives.

REFRESH TODAY'S PRIORITIES

His mercies are new every morning!

Are you following the Lord in everything you are doing? Is there something He has impressed you to do, a situation where you would be a godly influence on others, or a place He wants you to go that you are avoiding? Is there an issue in your life He is encouraging you to change, yet you are acting like you aren't hearing Him? Take a good, honest look at your life and allow the Holy Spirit to show you any area or issue where you are refusing to deny yourself and follow Jesus. Then repent and change it! You will not walk in the fullness of joy He has for you unless you take up your cross and follow Him.

PURIFIED DEVOTION

I want you to be free from concern. One who is unmarried is concerned about the things of the Lord, how he may please the Lord;

but one who is married is concerned about the things of the world, how he may please his wife,

and his interests are divided. The woman who is unmarried, and the virgin, is concerned about the things of the Lord, that she may be holy both in body and spirit; but one who is married is concerned about the things of the world, how she may please her husband.

This I say for your own benefit; not to put a restraint upon you, but to promote what is appropriate and to secure undistracted devotion to the Lord.

1 Corinthians 7:32-35 NASB

In verse 32 above, Paul expresses his desire that the saints in Corinth would be free of all worry and anxiety. Then he goes on to describe the cares and concerns of married people and unmarried people. He reminds us that married people have a priority that unmarried people do not have. Married people must consider their spouse as well as the Lord in everything they do, whereas unmarried people only have to consider the Lord.

In verse 35, Paul explains that he is not saying this to upset married people or to make them feel like they cannot serve the Lord as well as an unmarried person. He is simply giving them a reality check on keeping balance between the two. He's saying, "Whether you are married or not, maintain a secure, undistracted devotion to the Lord. If you put Him first in your relationship with your mate, your marriage will prosper along with the rest of your life."

We know God is not against marriage. He says in Hebrews 13:4 that marriage is honorable in all things. All things include our devotion to the Lord. Therefore, whether we are married or single, we can serve Him with all our heart, soul, mind and strength. We can have an intimate, wonderful relationship with God and with other people, especially our mate. The reality check Paul is giving us in this passage of Scripture is simply reminding us that our relationships should not distract us from our devotion to the Lord.

Paul also reminds us that the proper or "appropriate" perspective on relationships is that they are given to us by the Lord. He connects us in the body, and that includes our connection to our spouse. He leads us into every relationship involving our family, ministry, profession, neighbors and friends. All these relationships will only succeed and be enjoyable if they are conducted in the light of our primary relationship with Him.

If we are not careful, we can be distracted by all these other people in our lives, allowing their concerns and issues to draw our attention away from God, to get us sidetracked and even off the path He has us on. Jesus loved people and had great compassion on them, but He didn't follow them around and allow them to dictate His life. He followed the Holy Spirit and fulfilled the Word of God. His devotion to His Father was secure and undistracted at all times and in all situations. That is one reason He operated in perfect faith, peace and power.

When Jesus called the people to follow Him, He didn't mince words about the commitment He was asking them to make. He told them the truth and made it clear that following Him would mean He had to be number one in their lives.

> **There went great multitudes with him: and he turned, and said unto them,**
>
> **If any man come to me, and hate not his father, and mother, and wife, and children, and brethren, and sisters, yea, and his own life also, he cannot be my disciple.**
>
> **Luke 14:25-26**

Jesus was not commanding us to hate everybody but Him! He was telling us that our commitment to Him, our devotion to Him, must come before any other relationship. We are all soldiers in God's army, and when we enlist in the military and find ourselves on the battlefield, we cannot tell our commanding officer one day, "Oh, my wife called and I've got to go." We cannot look at Jesus one day and say, "Sorry, Lord, I've got to forget You and Your Word because I'm too busy dealing with the people at work. I have to please them, and I have to do what they want me to do."

We can play the church game, but we will never really get any results. If we are just going through the motions during Sunday and mid-week services, and ignoring the Lord and His Word the rest of the week, and are totally caught up in other people and other things, we will not live the abundant life He wants to give us. Jesus won't make a difference in our lives because we are not allowing Him to make a difference.

We can never be successful in any of our relationships if we don't give Jesus our secure, undistracted devotion. The only way anything in our lives will work properly is if we are abiding in Him. He said, "Without me ye can do nothing" (John 15:5). He also said that we must hate our own lives, which is another way of saying, "My true disciples are the ones who lose their life in Me. They set aside every selfish, self-centered thought and think only of Me and My will for their lives."

Jesus told it like it is when it came to serving Him. He gave us two examples of counting the cost of our commitment to Him.

> Which of you, intending to build a tower, sitteth not down first, and counteth the cost, whether he have sufficient to finish it?
>
> Lest haply, after he hath laid the foundation, and is not able to finish it, all that behold it begin to mock him,
>
> Saying, This man began to build, and was not able to finish.
>
> Or what king, going to make war against another king, sitteth not down first, and consulteth whether he be able with ten thousand to meet him that cometh against him with twenty thousand?
>
> Or else, while the other is yet a great way off, he sendeth an ambassage, and desireth conditions of peace.
>
> Luke 14:28-32

A contractor would be out of his mind not to figure out exactly what it was going to cost to build a building before he started working on it. Likewise, a king would be stupid to enter a war he knew his military was too weak and too ill-equipped to win. Jesus uses these examples to illustrate how we need to view our devotion to Him. When we look at our commitment to the Lord Jesus Christ, we should not be ignorant about the demands that commitment makes upon us.

Serving the Lord, consulting Him and doing His will in every situation, loving Him before anyone else in your life—will cost you something. You might be embarrassed when all your colleagues at work go out to a strip joint after work and you have to say, "Sorry, guys, I can't do that." The next morning you might overhear some of them laughing about what a church fool you are. Some of them may tell dirty jokes when you are around, forcing you to walk away. The devil will try to make you feel alone, rejected and isolated; but don't you believe it! You are taking a stand for Jesus and His righteousness, and only God knows the eternal impact you are having on their lives.

We must understand that if we want to see His transforming power at work in our lives and the lives of all we touch, serving the Lord cannot be half-hearted. What God wants is our whole heart. In prophesying of the new birth, Jeremiah declared how God sees it.

> **I will give them an heart to know me, that I am the LORD: and they shall be my people, and I will be their God: for they shall return unto me with their whole heart.**
>
> **Jeremiah 24:7**

The new birth itself is a picture of secure, undistracted devotion to the Lord. Being the disciple of Jesus is the greatest adventure a human being can have, but we have to forsake everything for Him to live that adventure to the fullest.

REFRESH TODAY'S PRIORITIES

His mercies are new every morning!

Today decide in your heart that your relationship with God is the most important relationship you have. He wants to spend time with you more than anyone else on this Earth. He loves you more than your spouse, your children, your family, your friends or your neighbors could ever love you. And He wants you to have the greatest life you can have. So spend the day with Him, not out of obligation but because you want to!

Day 38

YOUR NEW WARDROBE

Ye are all the children of God by faith in Christ Jesus.

For as many of you as have been baptized into Christ have put on Christ.

Galatians 3:26-27

The Bible tells us that the moment we were born again we "put on Christ." While the Holy Spirit baptized us into the Body of Christ, He also clothed us or wrapped us up in Christ. The Bible then instructs us to put on the new man, so putting on the new man must be a key to living a balanced life and a priority in our lives.

If so be that ye have heard him, and have been taught by him, as the truth is in Jesus:

That ye put off concerning the former conversation the old man, which is corrupt according to the deceitful lusts;

And be renewed in the spirit of your mind;

And that ye put on the new man, which after God is created in righteousness and true holiness.

Ephesians 4:21-24

Our old man serves the devil, the world, and every selfish whim and lust. Our new man serves Jesus, and the degree to which we serve Him and the excellence with which we serve Him depends on how much we renew our minds with His Word. Having a renewed mind is a great blessing! Everyone around us gets to enjoy the new man, the new us, the real us who is created in righteousness and true holiness—not a fake holiness that puts on spiritual airs and walks around bragging on how long we fasted and prayed this month, but a true holiness that comes from the love and truth of God inside us.

Since I have been on television with Creflo, I have had many new opportunities to decide whether I would put on the new man or stick with the old man! At Christmastime, not too long ago, I went into a store knowing exactly what I wanted. I found it and walked up to the lady at the cash register, wanting to pay for it quickly and be on my way. I could tell by the look on her face that she wasn't quite sure who I was, but she had an idea. Finally she said, "What's your name?"

My first thought was, *Oh, Jesus, here we go.* And with that stinky attitude I said, "Betty Price."

The woman looked very confused and said, "Ummm, Betty Price."

As she was ringing up my purchase, the Holy Ghost started to convict me, and I argued with Him a little. In my heart I was saying, *I don't want to tell her my name because then I'm going to have to get into talking about the church, hearing her testimony or her troubles, and I'm in a hurry.*

I knew I was wrong, that I shouldn't lie about who I really was, and that being in a hurry was no excuse for lying! I said, "I'm just joking. My name is Taffi Dollar." Then she smiled with relief and got real excited. The next thing I knew she picked up the phone and called all these extensions in the store to say, "Guess who's in the store? You won't believe it. Taffi Dollar's in the store." People started coming from all over the store to say hello and shake my hand. I took the time to hear their testimonies and listen to their stories, saying in my heart, "See, Lord, that's why I told her my name was Betty Price!" My heart was also laughing at myself because I had done the right thing. I had chosen to put on the new man, to be like Jesus, and those who spoke to me and shook my hand really blessed me that day.

Wherefore putting away lying, speak every man truth with his neighbour: for we are members one of another.

Be ye angry, and sin not: let not the sun go down upon your wrath:

Neither give place to the devil.

Ephesians 4:25-27

Putting on the new man is not always easy, but if we don't do it we will give place to the devil. If we lie or get angry and sin instead of forgiving and refusing to be offended, then it is just like we opened the door to Satan and all his demons and asked them to come in and torment us. Sometimes it seems like the devil sends people like that store clerk into our lives to tempt us to revert to the old man instead of putting on the new man. He knows that if he can get us to get back into that old suit of clothes, he can get us into big trouble and make our lives miserable.

Let no corrupt communication proceed out of your mouth, but that which is good to the use of edifying, that it may minister grace unto the hearers.

And grieve not the holy Spirit of God, whereby ye are sealed unto the day of redemption.

Ephesians 4:29-30

If we have ever grieved the Holy Spirit, then we never want to do it again! He is our Comforter, Teacher and Friend. He reveals Jesus, the Word and the heart of the Father, to us. The last thing in the world we want to do is grieve Him, just like a child never wants to cause their father or mother any pain or disappointment. But like children, there are times when each one of us allow some form of corrupt communication to come out of our mouths, which is what I did when I lied to the clerk in the store. Immediately, we feel the grief of the Holy Spirit inside us, and the best way to handle that is to repent immediately and do the right thing. I was blessed because eventually I made the right decision to put off that old man and put on the new man.

Lie not one to another, seeing that ye have put off the old man with his deeds;

And have put on the new man, which is renewed in knowledge after the image of him that created him.

Colossians 3:9-10

When we were saved, we put off the old man and his deeds, but sometimes a situation arises where that old man tries to take over again. The only way to get rid of him is to put on the new man and turn our attention back to Jesus, putting all our effort into getting to know Him better. Putting on the new man is another way of saying, "Put Jesus first. Walk in the Spirit. Abide in the Word."

REFRESH TODAY'S PRIORITIES

His mercies are new every morning!

This can be a very significant, special day for you if you choose to put on the new man whenever you find yourself feeling uncomfortable, tense, awkward, terrified, embarrassed, frustrated or infuriated. You see, when you choose to put on the new man and act like Jesus instead of being the old, unregenerated you, people will see Jesus instead of you. Those who have known the old you will ask you what has caused the difference! Those you could have hurt will be blessed instead. Putting on the new man in trying circumstances will always bring great blessing to you and to God's Kingdom, so make a commitment to put on the new man throughout your day.

Day 39

FREEDOM FRESHENER

But I say, walk and live [habitually] in the [Holy] Spirit
[responsive to and controlled and guided by the Spirit]; then
you will certainly not gratify the cravings and desires of the
flesh (of human nature without God).

For the desires of the flesh are opposed to the [Holy] Spirit,
and the [desires of the] Spirit are opposed to the flesh
(godless human nature); for these are antagonistic to each
other [continually withstanding and in conflict with each
other], so that you are not free but are prevented from doing
what you desire to do.

Galatians 5:16-17 AMP

I'm an intelligent person. I went to college, got my degree
and thought I was free doing my own thing. I thought I was
living in perfect balance and harmony with the universe. I was
the independent woman, not subject to anybody or anything,
and my concept of freedom was having the right to what I
thought was best, even if that meant rebelling against the
wishes of someone in authority. Therefore, when I got married,
I thought freedom was not doing what Creflo asked me to do.

After all, God gave me a mind, too, and I didn't need him to tell me how to live my life. I would say, "You're not my daddy!"

Was I happy, content and at peace? Did I *feel* balanced? No! I was in a constant struggle to get my own way, never really satisfied when I got it, and continuously convicted by the fact that I was not pleasing anyone—even myself. Deep inside, the Holy Spirit was telling me that something was very wrong.

Eventually I discovered that what was wrong was my idea of freedom. Real freedom is not the right to do anything you feel like doing, anytime you feel like doing it. Real freedom is found in conquering your flesh by serving God instead of yourself. You are truly free only when you are completely subjected to the Word of God, walking in the Spirit. Real freedom is a love walk that puts God first in all things. When you love God more than yourself, more than your selfish desires and dreams, more than your reputation, more than the love and respect of your family and friends, more than anyone or anything else in life—you find yourself truly free.

To get truly free I had to change my mind. I had to renew my mind to what the Word of God said and stop thinking like the world thought. I had to conquer my flesh by submitting my thoughts, my words and my actions to the Word of God, instead of doing whatever I felt like doing. That meant I had to look at my husband the way God told me to look at him. I had to see Creflo as God sees him. And I had to treat him the way God wanted me to treat him.

I read in my Bible, "Wives, submit yourselves unto your own husbands, as unto the Lord. For the husband is the head of the wife, even as Christ is the head of the church: and he is the saviour of the body. Therefore as the church is subject unto Christ, so let the wives be to their own husbands in every thing" (Ephesians 5:22-24). Immediately, my flesh rose up and said, "I can't believe you're going to submit to some man." The battle was on!

The greatest spiritual warfare you will ever do is right between your ears!

I was determined to put God's Word first in my life; that meant changing my mind about how I should treat my husband, especially when he did things that irritated me. I would get so angry with him because he would take my keys and put them where he put his keys. I'd be in a hurry to get somewhere and could not find my keys anywhere. He also didn't fill up the gas tank in the car until the warning light went on. So I would jump in the car to run to the store, pick up the kids at school and realize the light was on. I didn't know how long it had been on or if I had enough gas to get to the gas station.

At times like these, I have learned to cry out, "Help me, Jesus! I can't get in the flesh over this. I forgive Creflo and turn him over to You. You are the only One who can straighten him out!" When I'm cooled off and back in an attitude of love and respect, I can sit down with my husband and talk about these things. You see, I also read Ephesians 5:21, where it says we are to submit ourselves to one another in the fear of God. That means we need to talk to one another with the objective of working out our differences.

I know Creflo wants to be a godly husband and a blessing to me, but he can't do that if I never tell him what he can do to make my life easier. At the same time, he has to tell me a thing or two from time to time! I used to say to myself, "Oh no, Creflo's trying to put a strait jacket on me again." But as my mind was renewed by God's Word, I began to see that every time Creflo confronted me with something in my character or behavior that wasn't right, it was an opportunity to conquer my flesh and become more free. God was using my husband to get the strait jacket off me!

Now being made free from sin, and become servants to God, ye have your fruit unto holiness, and the end everlasting life.

Romans 6:22

Jesus freed us from sin and gave us the privilege of serving God instead of our flesh. When we understand this and begin to walk in it, we discover the tremendous joy of living for Him instead of ourselves. The ability and will to conquer sin is His gift of freedom to us. We experience real freedom mostly by dealing with the little things in life, like not being able to find our keys or running out of gas. These victories are not front-page news but are highly prized to us and to the Lord. Every time we conquer our flesh, He can use us in a more powerful way, entrust us with more responsibility in His Kingdom, and reveal more of His Word to us. Every piece of our flesh we subject to the Word and the Spirit glorifies Him.

We blame the devil for a lot of trouble that we cause ourselves. Truthfully, the devil can't do anything if we have our flesh under the control of the Word and the Spirit. A Believer who has conquered their flesh cannot be conquered by any enemy. When we are completely surrendered to the Lord, the enemy has no entrance into our lives. No matter what he does to attack us, he can never win.

We refuse to be offended and always forgive. We allow God to heal our hurts and deal with our attitudes. We are consumed with His Word, meditating in the truth day and night, casting down all vain or empty imaginations and making all thoughts line up with the Word. We do not let our emotions rule because we cast all our cares on the Lord and trust Him with every fear, offense and upset. When things don't happen the way we thought or hoped they would, we trust Him to work out all things for our good.

I thank God that one day in my walk with Him I decided to live by His Word and walk in His Spirit instead of doing my own thing. I look back on the independent woman I thought I was and laugh at my foolishness. I certainly wasn't happy, and I wasn't free either! I began to walk in true freedom when He became the Lord of every attitude, every thought, every word and every work in my life.

REFRESH TODAY'S PRIORITIES

His mercies are new every morning!

Today, you can be radically free if you will allow the Holy Spirit to deal with your flesh. If God is truly your first priority in life, then you must allow Him to show you those areas of your life that need to come under subjection to His Word and His Spirit. Just take one issue at a time. Don't get overwhelmed! And remember, you are His workmanship (Ephesians 2:10), and you are not alone in this. He will pick you up when you fall, set you back firmly on your feet, and take your hand to lead you into greater and greater freedom. From firsthand experience—but more importantly, from the authority of God's Word—I can promise you that you will be free as a soaring eagle if you conquer your flesh and live only for Him.

Choose the Beauty of a Balanced Life

I beseech you therefore, brethren, by the mercies of God, that ye present your bodies a living sacrifice, holy, acceptable unto God, which is your reasonable service.

And be not conformed to this world: but be ye transformed by the renewing of your mind, that ye may prove what is that good, and acceptable, and perfect, will of God.

Romans 12:1-2

We began this book talking about making choices, and we are ending by talking about making choices because God has ordained your life to be as balanced and wonderful tomorrow as the choices you make today. Some Christians believe that God is sovereign in the sense that He determines everything in our lives, but if that were the case, why did He give us a will to choose? Why does He command us to choose His way and His will in so many scriptures?

Living a balanced life by setting priorities comes down to choosing what is most important in your life. After choosing what is most important, then you find yourself making decisions moment by moment, day by day, in line with those priorities. If you have done the exercises at the end of each chapter, you have seen that your life becomes more and more balanced as you keep your priorities.

You have also discovered the benefit of setting godly priorities instead of worldly priorities. For example, the world says the body is the priority; give it whatever it wants. If it wants to have a milkshake or play tennis, or have sex, just do it! The world thinks it is silly to present your body to God as a living sacrifice; however, they don't understand the kind of life "living" means. Believers are alive to God! We have His life in us, and we give that life back to Him. So from moment to moment, we choose to live our lives for God instead of living for ourselves and the world.

The key to making the decision to present ourselves to God instead of serving our flesh is found in the word, transform. It comes from the Greek word *metamorphoo,* which is where we get the English word "metamorphosis." Someone or something that goes through a metamorphosis goes through a complete, inside-and-out change in character, condition, appearance or structure. This is why the word is translated "transform." It means a total change.

Romans 12:2 says that we are transformed by the "renewing of [the] mind." This means a complete renovation of our thinking, which we have talked about in this book. When our minds are renewed, we are God-conscious and can make choices in line with His will. We can prove His will by choosing to do things His way and watching the blessed results of that.

It isn't an accident that the butterfly is a great symbol of the Christian life. Before we are saved, we are like worms, crawling along the ground, not seeing where we are or where we are going, looking for anything we can find to keep us alive and make us happy. Then one day, the Holy Spirit begins to surround us with the saving power of God. Everywhere we turn, He is there, talking about Jesus, planting the Word of God in our hearts, and wrapping us up in His love and the dream that our lives could be different. Things get darker and darker as we see how black our hearts have become by sin, until one day the Holy Spirit has His way with us. He gives us a heart after God and out we come—beautiful, powerful and flying high!

This kind of transformation happened when we were born again, and it continues to happen as we put God and His Word before anything else. When getting to know Him is our first priority, everything else falls into place—and it all hangs on a simple choice. We can choose to crawl along the ground like we did before we knew Jesus, or we can choose to fly free like a butterfly in His Word and in His Spirit.

You will have many opportunities to make choices, and what you choose will either bring blessing or destruction into your life and possibly into the lives of those you touch. It all depends on what is most important to you. If Jesus truly is your Lord and not just your ticket to Heaven, if you really allow Him and His Word to rule your heart and mind, then I don't need to be a prophet to tell you that you will do great exploits for the Kingdom of God. You will lead a fulfilling, balanced life, and you will do it all with joy!

Refresh Today's Priorities

His mercies are new every morning!

Today, I want to give you a declaration to pray over yourself when you need a reminder of who you are in Jesus Christ and how He is the most important One in your life. Think about what you're saying. Listen to what you're saying. Don't just go through the motions. Allow these words to take root in your mind and capture your heart.

Father, thank You for saving me, healing me, setting me free, and loving me as Your precious child. You are my Father, and You are the Father of spirits, so I am a spirit. Thank You that today I am spiritually alive to You, I live in a body that is Your temple, and my soul is renewed and transformed by Your Word. I love Your Word and meditate on it, always. I study Your Word and achieve great success in every area of my life. Thank You, Father, that Your Holy Spirit teaches me, comforts me and guides me with Your truth. He gives direction to my spirit and illumination to my mind. He leads me in the way that I should go in all the affairs of life. And He gives me the wisdom and the strength to overcome every temptation, fault, weakness and sin. In Jesus Christ, Your love is perfected in me and I have an unction from the Holy One who lives in me. My life today is joy unspeakable and full of glory because I choose to love You and serve You first! In the mighty name of Jesus I pray. Amen.

Prayer of Salvation

God loves you—no matter who you are, no matter what your past. God loves you so much that He gave His one and only begotten Son for you. The Bible tells us that "…whoever believes in him shall not perish but have eternal life" (John 3:16 NIV). Jesus laid down His life and rose again so we could spend eternity with Him in Heaven and experience His absolute best on Earth. If you would like to receive Jesus into your life, say the following prayer out loud and mean it from your heart:

Heavenly Father, I come to You admitting that I am a sinner. Right now, I choose to turn away from sin, and I ask You to cleanse me of all unrighteousness. I believe that Your Son, Jesus, died on the cross to take away my sins. I also believe that He rose again from the dead so that I might be forgiven of my sins and made righteous through faith in Him. I call upon the name of Jesus Christ to be the Savior and Lord of my life. Jesus, I choose to follow You and ask that You fill me with the power of the Holy Spirit. I declare that right now I am a child of God. I am free from sin and full of the righteousness of God. I am saved in Jesus' name. Amen.

If you prayed this prayer to receive Jesus Christ as your Savior for the first time, please contact us on the Web at **harrisonhouse.com** to receive a free book.

Or you may write to us at

Harrison House
P.O. Box 35035
Tulsa, OK 74153

ABOUT THE AUTHOR

Taffi L. Dollar is a world-renowned author, teacher and conference speaker who demonstrates God's love to others. As the wife of Dr. Creflo A. Dollar, she co-pastors World Changers Church International (WCCI) in College Park, Georgia, and World Changers Church-New York.

A minister of the Gospel, Taffi has a global influence in both ministry and music. She serves as the CEO of Arrow Records, a cutting-edge Christian recording company.

Taffi's commitment to helping others is evident through her lifestyle of service. She founded the Women's Ministry at WCCI to promote unity and sisterhood. In addition, Taffi founded the World Changers Christian Academy Independent Study Program (ISP), an alternative to traditional home schooling. Taffi also serves as an active mentor and sponsor of the Service to Education program at Toney Elementary School in Decatur, Georgia, where she plays an instrumental role in helping students to excel in reading.

With a bachelor's degree in mental health and human services, Taffi has a heart for restoring family relationships. Above all her accomplishments, she considers supporting her husband in ministry and raising godly children her primary purpose. As a mother of five, she firmly believes that the best way to raise successful children is to be an active role model in demonstrating the love of God.

To contact Taffi L. Dollar, please write to:

Creflo Dollar Ministries

P.O. Box 490124

College Park, GA 30349

Or call

(866) 477-7683

Or go online to her Web site

creflodollarminstries.com

Fast. Easy. Convenient.

For the latest Harrison House product information and author news, look no further than your computer. All the details on our powerful, life-changing products are just a click away. New releases, E-mail subscriptions, Podcasts, testimonies, monthly specials—find it all in one place. Visit harrisonhouse.com today!

harrisonhouse

The Harrison House Vision

Proclaiming the truth and the power

Of the Gospel of Jesus Christ

With excellence;

Challenging Christians to

Live victoriously,

Grow spiritually,

Know God intimately.